# Render Unto Darwin

# Books by James H. Fetzer

# Render Unto Darwin

*Philosophical Aspects of the
Christian Right's
Crusade Against Science*

JAMES H. FETZER

OPEN COURT
Chicago and La Salle, Illinois

To order books from Open Court, call toll-free 1-800-815-2280, or visit our website at www.opencourtbooks.com.

Open Court Publishing Company is a division of Carus Publishing Company.

**Library of Congress Cataloging-in-Publication Data**

Fetzer, James H., 1940-
    Render unto Darwin : philosophical aspects of the Christian right's crusade against science / James H. Fetzer.
        p.    cm.
        Summary: "Examines philosophical issues underlying controversial topics in modern science such as abortion, stem-cell research, human cloning, evolution, creationism, and intelligent design. Also evaluates the merit of different conceptions of morality, coming down in favor of a deonotological ethical standard and against the standards of evangelical Christianity and the political right"—Provided by publisher.
        Includes bibliographical references and index.
        ISBN-13: 978-0-8126-9605-9 (trade paper : alk. paper)
        ISBN-10: 0-8126-9605-0 (trade paper : alk. paper)  1. Religion and science.
    2. Christian conservatism—United States  3. Christianity and politics—United States  4. United States—Church history  I. Title.
    BL240.3.F48 2007
    261.5'50973—dc22                                                         2006036617

For Bret

*And he saith unto them, Render therefore unto Caesar the things which are Caesar's; and unto God the things which are God's.*

—Matthew 22:21

# Contents

# Figures and Tables

# *Preface*

I am a philosopher of science. In this book I look closely at particular issues in religion and politics which have to do with science. These issues arise because of the political aims and activities of the Christian Right.

I have been fascinated by articles of faith since my youth, when I was exposed to the doctrine of the Trinity—the Father, the Son, and the Holy Ghost—which left me wondering whether Christians believed in one god or three. That proved to be only the first of the puzzles religious belief has posed for me, especially as I became more and more familiar with science.

The chapters that follow address the extent to which science and religion are capable of reconciliation. They examine the case for Creationism in its various forms, as contrasted with evolutionary theory, with particular reference to what counts as genuine science.

I also look into the moral claims of the Christian Right, as these relate to such matters as abortion and stem-cell research. This leads me to compare various theories of morality, and to conclude that only one of these theories is adequate. A deontological conception of morality, requiring that we treat other persons with respect and never merely as means, emerges from my analysis. Applying this theory, I conclude that prohibitions against prostitution, smoking pot, or burning flags are unjustified. Abortion, stem-cell research, and cloning deserve to be regulated, but are not in themselves necessarily immoral.

In my view, the Right is an unholy alliance between those serving the interests of the rich and various religious and moral views which are in themselves of no interest to the rich, but do offer a convenient political strategy for cementing their grip on political power. My conclusion is the rather bleak one that we are witnessing a new, American-style form of fascism which threatens to strangle freedom and democracy—in the name of freedom and democracy.

In addition to drawing upon several of my lesser writings without explicit acknowledgment, I have used material from some longer studies in Chapter 5, namely: 'The Ethics of Belief: Taking Religion out of Public Policy Debates', *Bridges* 11: 3–4 (2004); and *Computers and Cognition: Why Minds Are Not Machines* (Dordrecht: Kluwer, 2002); and, in the Appendix, 'Transcendent Laws and Empirical Procedures', in N. Rescher, ed., *The Limits of Lawfulness* (Pittsburgh: University Press of America, 1983), pp. 25–32.

Those who would like to pursue the issues involved in accounting for consciousness, cognition, and mentality within an evolutionary framework might like to read my earlier work, *The Evolution of Intelligence: Are Humans the Only Animals with Minds?* (Chicago: Open Court, 2005). That book, offering a study in the emergence of crucial properties that distinguish Homo sapiens from other animal species, is complementary to this one.

This book, more so than any other of mine, has benefited from collaboration with my editor, David Ramsay Steele, whom I have come to admire for his keen intellect, excellent judgment, and patient manner. Having already published four books with him, it is a great pleasure to formally acknowledge my indebtedness to him.

# Glossary of Terms Used
# in This Book

**Abductivism.** Conception of science as a process of puzzlement, speculation, adaptation, and explanation, whose basic rule of reasoning is inference to the best explanation.

**Agnosticism.** Belief neither in the existence of God nor in the non-existence of God.

**Algorithm.** an effective decision procedure such that, in relation to a fixed class of problems, it is always applicable, always yields a correct solution, and does so in a finite sequence of steps.

**Analytic truths.** Sentences that are true on the basis of their grammar and their meaning alone, such as 'Bachelors are unmarried' and 'Roses are flowers'.

**Artificial selection.** Deliberate intervention to affect reproductive behavior, such as by artificial insemination, arranged marriages, and stud farms.

**Atheism.** Belief in the non-existence of God.

**Big Bang model.** The universe had a beginning with the Big Bang, which brought about an expansion that may produce a mass-energy soup (George Gamow).

**Christian Fundamentalism.** Religious movement rooted in a literal interpretation of the Bible.

**Class.** A collection of things, no matter how heterogeneous. A class could even, for instance, comprise an old comb, the square root of $-1$, and the President of the US.

**Classic creationism.** Three versions. (CC-1) God created the world and all life exactly as it exists today; (CC-2) God created the world and all life in forms that are fixed and unchanging; and (CC-3) God create the world and all life using the causal mechanisms of evolution.

**Classic utilitarianism.** An action A is right when it produces at least as much net happiness for everyone as any available alternative.

**Closed systems.** Systems for which every value of every variable affecting their behavior is specified (thus satisfying the requirement of maximal specificity).

**Conditional.** A sentence of 'if . . . then . . .' form. There are several kinds, including material, subjunctive, causal, and probabilistic causal conditionals.

**Consciousness.** The ability to use signs of specific kinds; hence, consciousness is properly consciousness-relative-to-signs-of-kind-S.

**Conspecifics.** Members of the same species.

**Creation Science.** The Earth was created about ten thousand years ago in approximately the complexity it displays today; micro-evolution is possible but not macro-evolution; there was a world-wide flood about five thousand years ago.

**Creationism.** Belief that God created the world, which assumed different forms as traditional Creationism, classic Creationism (in three versions), Creation Science (defined by three theses), and Intelligent Design.

**Cultural relativism.** An action A is right (in culture C) if C approves of A.

Deductivism. Conception of science as a process of conjecture, derivation, experimentation, and elimination, whose basic rule of reasoning is *modus tollens*.

**Deism.** The belief that God, usually not a person, created the universe but does not intervene in its history.

**Deontological moral theory.** An action A is right when it involves treating other persons as ends (or valuable in themselves) and never merely as means.

**Determinism.** Locally, same cause, same effect; universally, all processes (laws) are deterministic.

**Empirical truths.** Sentences that are true but not on the basis of their grammar and their meaning alone, such as 'Bill is a bachelor' and 'Some roses are red'.

**Entropy.** The tendency of systems toward dissipation of matter-energy toward states of equal distribution (maximal stability).

**Ethical egoism.** An action A is right (for person P) if P approves of A.

**Ethical egoism.** An action A is right for (for person P) when it produces at least as much happiness for P as any available alternative.

**Extensional distributions.** Constant conjunctions or relative frequencies between properties or events during the world's history that might possibly be violated or might possibly be changed. *See* Universal law, Statistical law.

**Extensions.** Classes of things that satisfy the intensions specified by definitions of kinds of things, when they are homogeneous; but extensions include the members of collections of things that may share no properties in common.

**Family values.** An action A is right (for family F) if F approves of A.

**First Cause.** The history of the world as a series of effects is either infinite or had a first effect; but it cannot be infinite; therefore, it had a first effect and the cause of that first effect is known as the 'First Cause' (which is identified with God).

**Frequency interpretation of probability.** Probabilities are identified with the relative frequencies of outcomes of certain kinds within finite sequences or the limiting frequencies of those same outcomes within infinite sequences (how often things happen).

**Genetic drift.** Changes in gene pools brought about by adaptive pressures when different sub-populations of an original population are subjected to different environment, which brought about the emergence of races.

**Genetic engineering.** The use of engineering techniques to effect changes in genes and their combination, including stem-cell research and cloning.

**Genetic mutation.** Changes that occur when genes of one kind are changed into genes of another kind by natural causes like cosmic rays.

**Genome.** The complete set of genes for a species, including those for phenotypic properties, such as being male or female, African or Oriental, that may or may not occur together.

**Genotype.** The combinations of genes that tends to give rise to a specific phenotype.

**Group selection.** The adaptive benefits of different arrangements of sets of conspecifics, such as the members of a rifle team organized as a platoon.

**Gullibility.** Subjective tendency to accept or believe that varies from person to person and from time to time.

**Harm principle.** It is morally wrong to inflict physical harm upon persons without their consent.

**Iconic mentality.** The ability to use icons, which are signs that resemble what they stand for.

**Indeterminism.** Locally, same cause, one or another within a fixed set of possible effects; globally, at least one process (law) is indeterministic.

**Indexical mentality.** The ability to use indices, which are signs that are causes or effects of that for which they stand.

**Inductivism.** Conception of science as a process of observation, classification, generalization, and prediction, whose basic rule of reasoning is the straight rule.

**Instrumentalism.** The entities and processes posited by a theory need not exist or be real as long as the theory functions successfully as a predictive device.

**Intelligent Design.** The world was created by an intelligent designer, which is proven by the existence of irreducible complexity.

**Intensional generalizations.** Generalizations specifying what would happen or be the case if something were to happen or be the case, which are typically expressed by means of subjunctive or of causal conditionals.

**Intensions.** Conditions that must be satisfied for something to be a thing of a specific kind, as a chair is a surface suitable for sitting by one person and man-made.

**Laws of nature.** Generalizations specifying what would happen or be the case if something (else) were to happen or be the case, characterized by means of subjunctive or causal conditionals of universal or of probabilistic strength.

**Limited utilitarianism.** An action A is right (for group G) when it produces at least as much happiness for G as any available alternative.

**Long-run.** Sequences that are infinite by virtue of having no end.

**Macro-evolution.** Changes (variations) that qualify as constituting the emergence of new species from previously existing species or the extinction of that species.

**Mentality.** The capacity to use signs.

**Micro-evolution.** Changes (variations) within existing species that do not qualify as constituting the emergence of a new species or the extinction of that species.

**Monotheism.** The belief that there exists one and only one god.

**Natural selection.** In its narrow sense, competition between conspecifics for food, shelter, and other resources that contribute to survival; in its broad sense, any of the eight causal mechanisms of biological evolution.

**Open systems.** Systems for which the values of some variables affecting their behavior is unspecified (thus failing the requirement of maximal specificity).

**Optimizing.** Processes or procedures are optimizing when they produce 'the best possible' outcome or result.

**Pantheism.** The belief that God and Nature are one and the same.

**Phenotype.** The specific properties of the bodies and brains of specific organisms.

**Pleiotropic effects.** Multiple phenotypic effects brought about by single genes.

**Polygenic interactions.** Phenotypic effects that are brought about by the causal interaction of two or more genes.

**Polytheism.** The belief that more than one god exists, possibly many.

**Prime Mover.** The history of the world as a series of motions is either infinite or had a first movement; but it cannot be infinite; therefore, it had a first movement and the cause of that first movement is known as the 'Unmoved Mover' or as the 'Prime Mover' (which is identified with God).

**Probability.** Ambiguous term for measuring the weight of evidence, the frequency of outcomes, the strength of causal tendency, and so on.

**Problem of Evil.** If God is omniscient, omnipotent, and omnibenevolent, then why are there so many bad things in the world, like plagues, wars, and famines?

**Program.** The encoding of an algorithm in a form suitable for execution by a machine.

**Propensity interpretation of probability.** Probabilities are identified with the strength of causal tendency for an event of one kind to bring about an event of another, where a short or long run is a sequence of single cases (how strongly it is brought about).

**Property.** Loosely, a trait, feature, or characteristic of things; strictly, a single-case dispositional tendency, where everything that has the same property has the same dispositions that attending having that property, such as the tendency of things that are round to roll on an inclined plane and of things that are elastic to give when bent, where kinds are defined by properties.

**Rationality.** Subjective tendency to accept or believe that satisfies objective standards of logic and evidence.

**Realism.** The entities and processes posited by theories must exist and be real if those theories are to be capable of explaining as well as predicting experience.

**Religious ethics.** An action A is right (for religion R) if R approves of A.

**Rules of thumb.** Usually correct but not therefore infallible guides to right action.

**Satisficing.** Processes or procedures are satisficing when they produce outcomes or results that are 'good enough', even if other outcomes or results might be better.

**Sentience.** The capacity to experience sensations, especially pain.

**Sexual reproduction.** The process of combining genes from the male and the female of the species to produce an offspring through sexual intercourse.

**Sexual selection.** The preference of members of one sex for members of the opposite sex based upon specific phenotypic traits.

**Short-run.** Sequences that are finite by virtue of having an end.

**Single-case.** Individual events that could comprise a sequences.

**Social contract theory.** An action A is right for society S when it has been agreed upon by the members of society S.

**Specious bifurcation.** Begging the question by dividing an issue into two mutually exclusive and jointly exhautive alternatives, when there are many additional but suppressed alternatives.

**Statistical law.** In its weak sense, a statistical law reflects a relative frequency between properties or events during the world's history; in its strong sense, a probabilistic connection that cannot be violated and cannot be changed. See also Indeterminism.

**Steady State model.** The universe has no beginning and no end, where matter and energy are subject to local but not to universal variation (Fred Hoyle).

**Symbolic mentality.** The ability to use symbols, which are signs that are merely habitually associated with that for which they stand.

**Tautology.** Sentence that cannot be false because its truth is guaranteed by its meaning alone ('Bachelors are unmarried', 'Roses are flowers').

**Tentative.** A belief, conclusion, or viewpoint is tentative when it might be abandoned, rejected, or revised on the basis of additional evidence.

**Testable.** A conjecture, hypothesis, or theory is testable when it can be subjected to tests on the basis of observation, experiment, or measurement.

**Theism.** Belief in the existence of God.

**Theory.** In its loose sense, any conjecture, speculation, or guess; in its strict sense, a potentially explanatory lawlike hypothesis or a set of hypotheses of this kind.

**Traditional creationism.** The world as a Creation had a supernatural Creator.

**Universal law.** In its weak sense, a universal law reflects a constant conjunction between properties or events during the world's history; in its strong sense, a constant conjunction that cannot be violated and cannot be changed *See also* Determinism.

**Viability.** Survivability independently of any womb, natural or artificial.

PROLOGUE

# Going by the Book

- *Science perpetually revises itself, whereas religion usually resists revision*
- *Religion focuses on precise words, but these words may be interpreted differently*
- *In the beginning . . .? There may have been no beginning*
- *The Big Bang may be an episode in an endless cycle without beginning and without end*
- *Life gains in complexity while the Cosmos grows more chaotic*

*In the beginning was the Word, and the Word was with God, and the Word was God.* (John 1:1)

Science and religion are different in many ways. One of these is that they typically take a different attitude toward their beliefs and assertions. Scientific hypotheses and theories are conditional in their form, testable in their content, and subject to revision with the accumulation of additional relevant evidence. Religious teachings are typically unconditional in their form, untestable in their content, and held without reservation, come what may.

Science is always somewhat tentative and expects to revise itself continually. Religion tends to resist revision, holding that some of the insights it has gained are certain and beyond question. They qualify as 'articles of faith', requiring no support based on observations, measurements, or experiment. And yet they tend to be held with absolute conviction, a kind of certainty that even extends to the very meaning of the written word. In religion, it's often considered praiseworthy to have faith, whereas for one scientist to urge another to have faith in a particular theory would make little sense.

Religion is always focused on precise words. Words matter greatly to religious people, and they matter greatly to philosophers for a somewhat different reason. We typically use words to talk about things in the world, but sometimes we use them to talk about words themselves. In order to circumvent confusion on this score, philosophers and linguists place a word within quotation marks to make it conspicuous that the word itself is under consideration. This is known as the 'use-mention' distinction. Unless John 1:1 was intended to suggest that God is merely a word, it should read, "In the beginning was the Word, and the Word was with God, and the Word was 'God'". First-century Greek writers did not use quotation marks in that way, so we can't be sure whether that captures the intention, or whether something else was meant.

## 0.1 *When Words Fail*

There are enduring differences even over the very words on the page. The quotation from John 1:1 cited above is the same as that found in the King James Version, the American Standard Version, the J.N. Darby Translation of 1890, the World English Bible, and others still. But if they always used the same words in the same order, different translations would be redundant. The Bible in Basic English, for example, translates this text: "From the first he was the Word, and the Word was in relation with God and was

God". This, alas, makes the distinction between 'God' as the name and God as the thing named hopelessly obscure. If God was the Word and the Word was God, as this translation implies, then apparently the thing and the word are one and the same. If few theologians would find that satisfactory as a doctrine, how could the man in the street possibly make heads or tails of it?

Moreover, the Bible has been translated into many different languages, from Korean to Xhosa, not to mention English. You don't have to be a linguist to recognize that the precise meaning attached to John 1:1 in various different languages almost surely varies from case to case. When a believer affirms that she believes in the Bible, what does that mean when in comes to John 1:1, for example? I am a professional philosopher; the meaning of words is my stock in trade. Philosophers sort out ambiguities and vagueness in language all the time. But if I were pressed as to the meaning of this passage, I would express very great uncertainty. I find it difficult to be sure just what it's supposed to mean.

Now John 1:1 may be an exception with regard to its explicit invocation of the notion of a word in relation to the existence of God. But there are plenty of other examples that raise more serious problems. Some Muslims, it is said, believe that if they become martyrs for the faith, then they will receive the eternal reward of having seventy-two virgins to themselves in the afterlife. Presumably these consorts won't remain virgins for long, unless they are replaced every few days. Some scholars of the Quran, however, have suggested that the key word has been mistranslated. According to these scholars, when the old Arabic word 'hur' is accurately rendered, what awaits these young men who die for a sacred cause is not seventy-two 'virgins' but seventy-two 'white grapes'. If this becomes generally known, there might be fewer suicide bombers.

Words matter. The Old Testament was written in Hebrew and the New Testament in Greek. The gospels of Matthew and Luke say that Jesus was miraculously born to Mary, a virgin. This is said to be a fulfillment of the Old Testament prophecy in Isaiah 7:14, predicting that "a virgin shall conceive, and bear a son." We can see that the writers of the New Testament did not have the Old Testament books in the original Hebrew, nor in Aramaic, but only in a Greek translation. For Isaiah 7:14 asserts that "a young woman [Hebrew *almah*] shall conceive and bear a son." "Young woman" was translated into Greek as "virgin" [Greek *parthenos*]. Matthew and Luke, or whoever wrote the gospels that were much later given these names, may have been misled by a simple mistranslation.

Even the history of the creation of the written Bible turns out to be complex, dependent upon its preservation by means of an oral tradition, before it was reduced to writing in Hebrew and Greek. Who knows what subtle transformations may have crept into that tradition during the decades before these events were committed to writing, or may have crept in to the text later as these works were copied out repeatedly by scribes? (For a fascinating introduction to some of these issues, as applied to the New Testament, see Ehrman 2005. See also Wells 1999.)

Debate has arisen over whether the Quran is more historical, more reliable, less legendary, than the Bible. The standard account is that the Quran was given to the world by the prophet Muhammad, who lived from A.D. 570 to 632. Muhammad was commanded by the angel Gabriel to "Recite!" and did so in a kind of fit that fell upon him frequently for a period of twenty-three years until his death. His recitations were allegedly memorized by some of his followers, and in some cases scraps of them were written down. In the decades after his death, attempts were made to collect together all the various versions of bits and pieces of recitation which had been recorded, which were edited together to make the Quran. Variant versions were destroyed by the Caliph Umar in order to produce a single holy book without confusing rivals.

In the ancient world, it was commonplace to collect together wise or inspired sayings and attribute them to legendary great figures from the past. The earliest surviving account of the life of Muhammad is by Ibn Hisham, who died in A.D. 834, two hundred years after the date ascribed to the death of the Prophet. Ibn Hisham's biography incorporates edited material from an earlier biography, now lost, by Ibn Ishaq, written around 750. So it would not be wrong to say we have access to an account of Muhammad's life from 128 years after the presumptive date of his death. This is more than ample time for legends to proliferate (see Ibn Warraq 1995; 2000). But while many legends did proliferate during that time, the prevailing view among scholars is that the integrity of the Quran was preserved largely intact and that the early histories of Ibn Hisham and Ibn Ishaq are generally reliable. However, no contemporary records of Muhammadd or of the generation of the Quran have survived. Contrary to the view of Muslims and of the majority of scholars, revisionist scholars maintain that Muhammad is an obscure legendary figure about whom almost nothing is known for certain.

The literary qualities of the Quran are widely admired by its followers but have been disputed by critics. Most commentators take it to represent a unified, single point of view.

Even given the 'final' version of the Quran available today, difficulties of interpretation have arisen. Written Arabic omitted the vowels, and this left open the possibility of alternative readings, with quite different meanings, in a number of places. While today there are officially fourteen ways to read the Quran, there is wide agreement among Muslims that the text is not capable of adequate translation and the Arabic original is the only version that can be relied on. Most Muslims feel they need to learn to read Arabic in order to read the Quran. Few Christians, other than ordained ministers, ever learn Hebrew or Greek to better understand the Bible.

The Quran contains many modified and variant versions of Jewish and Christian traditions. Among them, the Quran agrees that Jesus was born of a virgin. So nearly all Muslims accept the virgin birth of Jesus, while many Christians have their doubts on this score. A virgin birth, in the absence of modern biological techniques, would have been humanly impossible. It's difficult to see why anyone should be disposed to accept the accounts of the authors of 'Matthew' and 'Luke', writing in Greek, about sixty years after the approximate date of Mary's pregnancy. Had these authors, sixty years earlier, in a different country, with a different language, been keeping Mary under such close observation that they were in a position to give testimony, solid enough to satisfy a court of law, that she had not had sex with any human male? The virgin birth looks like a typical case of elaborated legend. Paul, writing in the 50s A.D., well before the composition of the gospels, knows nothing of it.

A further example of the difficulties of interpreting the written word is the Biblical account of the Creation. According to Genesis 1:2, God created day and night on the first day, but according to Genesis 1:14–19, God only got around to creating the Sun and the Moon on the fourth day, which generates the quandary of how day and night existed prior to the creation of the Sun and the Moon. Similarly, according to Genesis 1:27, God created man and woman together "in his own image" yet, according to Genesis 2:21–22, God put the first man, Adam, into a deep sleep and took out a rib, from which he fashioned the first woman, Eve.

Both accounts can hardly be true. If God created both sexes at the same time, then God cannot have first created man, put him into a deep sleep, and then created woman. Alternatively, if God first created man, put him into a deep sleep and then created woman, he cannot have created them both at the same time. Priests and theologians have come up with attempts to reconcile the words found in Genesis, but on a literal reading, the Bible cannot be reconciled with itself, and so some considerable degree of interpretation is required to render it consistent.

If Adam and Eve were the only humans created by God, and Able, Cain, and Seth were their only offspring, as Genesis 4:1–2 and Genesis 5:4 maintain, then where did the rest of humanity come from? We are not talking about virgin births here, but the seemingly evident necessity that humanity may have been conceived by the sin of incest.

There are alternatives, of course, where Genesis 5:2, for example, could be interpreted to mean that God made Adam and Eve and then made many other males and females. But the point is that all of this requires interpretation, not literal acceptance. Even the story of creation over six days (after which God 'rested' on the seventh), taken literally, cannot be reconciled with the known age of Earth, which is around four and a half billion years. If you indulge the conceit of translating the meaning of "day" in the English translations of ancient texts, however, it may be possible to reconcile them. Assume, for example, that each Biblical 'day' is a billion years. Then the Biblical record of creation over six billion years is a fair approximation to the findings of astronomy, geology, and archaeology.

In order to attain that reconciliation, it was necessary to abandon the literal interpretation of the text. The Roman Catholic Church does not encounter these difficulties, because it has never committed itself to purely literal interpretation, and now adheres to the position that God could have created the universe using evolution as His mechanism. Catholic thinkers as early as Augustine allowed that the 'days' of Genesis were probably not literal days, but much longer time periods. Some scientists and historians of science contend that the emergence of science as a Western phenomenon was facilitated by the conception of God as the lawgiver who created the universe governed by laws. The discovery of those laws is therefore part and parcel of the discovery of God's will. In this fashion, the Church has found a way to reconcile evolution with theology by rendering unto God that which is God's and unto Darwin that which is Darwin's.

## 0.2 *Was There a Beginning?*

*In the beginning God created the heaven and the earth.* (Genesis 1:1)

If God created the heaven and the earth, then it might be a mistake to try to understand the world and its origin exclusively on the basis of science, because complete understanding would require knowledge of an act of creation by God. Among the first lessons of a scientific education, however, is that no one can subject a hypothesis to appropriate tests without understanding what it means—if not exactly in every detail, then at least enough to know what to observe or measure. The hypothesis that God created the heaven and the earth appears to be sufficiently intelligible in relation to the heavens above us and the earth beneath our feet, but what of God? What does 'God' mean?

If the name 'God' refers to an old man who lives on a mountain and dispenses advice, then God is clearly finite and fallible. If it refers to the Old Testament conception, then God is not only very powerful but also emotionally excitable, capricious in his attachments, and rather intrusive in human affairs, often preoccupied with punishment and revenge. If it refers to the New Testament conception, then this God, seen from some angles, is a loving and merciful figure, who represents forgiveness and compassion, though there is a prominent place in his Creation for eternal torment in Hell. More abstractly, God may be defined as omniscient, omnipotent, omnipresent, and omnibenevolent.

That is the classic God of Christian and Muslim theology, but it is difficult to fit Him into those other conceptions. There are also pantheism, deism, or polytheism. Pantheists identify God with the whole universe. Deists think of God as impersonal and non-interventionist. Polytheists believe in many Gods. Buddhism accepts the existence of powerful god-like figures known as 'devas', who have little to do with humans, but rejects the notion of a God who created the universe.

The God of classical theism still prevails among theologians. God is an omniscient, omnipotent, non-material, and completely benevolent being, whom we ought to worship and obey. A serious difficulty for classical theism is Problem of Evil, which arises because of the presence of so many bad things in the world, such as disease, pestilence, and famine. If God knows everything and can do anything, why should there be evil in the world? And so much of it. It's difficult to avoid the conclusion that if there is a God, He is not omnipotent, or not omnisicient, or not all-loving.

Some religions, such as Confucianism, emphasize moral principles and right conduct, while others, such as Taoism and Buddhism, place emphasis upon contemplation or focus upon the cessation of desire, respectively. Many religions, such as Islam and Hinduism, embrace combinations of monotheism and social practices, such as prayer, fasting, almsgiving and pilgrimages, in the first instance, and a rigid system of social castes, in the second. Islam promises Paradise for the faithful and Hell for infidels, while Hinduism accepts the existence of Brahma, the primal cause and pervading spirit of the universe.

If, in the beginning, some kind of God or gods created heaven and earth, then there are numerous candidates for that role. But actually, there did not have to be a beginning. Some things have no beginning. Consider the series of negative integers that ends with the number zero:

$$\ldots -4, -3, -2, -1, 0.$$

This is a sequence that has no first member and thus has no beginning. And some things have no end. Consider the series of positive integers that begins with the number zero in a sequence generated by adding one to each member:

$$0, 1, 2, 3, 4, \ldots$$

This is a sequence that has no last member and thus has no end. Indeed, some things have neither a beginning nor an end. Consider the series of positive and negative integers when they are joined by using zero as a point of intersection:

$$\ldots -3, -2, -1, 0, 1, 2, 3, \ldots$$

This sequence is a series of integers that has no first member and no last. But if some things have no beginning and no end, it must be imaginable for things to exist without having a beginning and even without having an end. So perhaps the world that consists of heaven and earth had no beginning and has no end.

The objection could be lodged that numbers and worlds are different kinds of things, like apples and oranges, which might be similar in some respects but nonetheless differ. Numbers, for example, are abstract things that are not even in space and time, unlike the numerals we use to name or describe them. This becomes obvious in the case of numbers such as pi and the square root of -1. Pi, for example, as the ratio of the circumference of a circle to its diameter, has an infinite (non-terminating and non-repeating) decimal numerical representation beginning with the sequence, 3.14159265 . . . . Having no last digit, the complete decimal expansion for pi cannot even be written down in space and time.

Numbers can be named or described in many different systems of notation, Arabic (0, 1, 2, 3, . . . ) and Roman (I, II, III, . . . ) being only the most familiar. The number named by the Arabic numeral "2" and by the Roman numeral "II" is the same number, which—in other contexts—might likewise be indicated by raising two fingers of your right hand, as in the case of umpires calling strikes. Perhaps numerals, like fingers and hands, as physical things in space and time, had to have a beginning and have to have an end. Since they are things in the world, perhaps the world considered as a totality in space and time—as everything physical there is, was or will be (present, past or future)—is like them in this respect and therefore had to have a beginning and also has to have an end.

This question matters to non-scientists and scientists alike, because if heaven and earth had no beginning and have no end, there might be no role for God to play in creating them and alternatively no 'first moment' for science to explain. Just because certain abstract entities such as some sequences of numbers have no beginning and no end, after all, does not show that physical entities such as heaven and earth might have no beginning and no end. Scientists have diverged in their opinions about this matter, where among the best known theories of the origins of the universe in the past have been the Steady State model proposed by Fred Hoyle (1950) and the Big Bang model advanced by George Gamow (1954). For the purpose of consideration within this context, only a few of their more general features require attention here.

## 0.3  *Two Models of the Universe.*

According to the Big Bang model, the world had a beginning in time initiated by a primordial explosion that occurred when all of its mass and all of its energy was condensed into a virtually infinitesimal point at enormously high temperature. The immense force of this explosion was sufficiently great to overcome the force of gravity that draws together everything having mass, while conditions that are sufficient for the formation of hydrogen, helium, and other elements were realized—even during the first three minutes! According to the Steady State model, by comparison, the world had no beginning in time but persists today in a Steady State of creation that depends on the continuous production of hydrogen and other elements condensing into stars and galaxies, which occurs at roughly the same rate that stars and galaxies are extinguished.

It may look as though a Steady State model imposes no beginning in time upon the universe, while Big Bang models do. What actually had to have a beginning in time on the Big Bang model, however, may be better envisioned as single cycles in an endless sequence of cycles and recycles. The expansion of matter and energy precipitated by the Big Bang may, theoretically, at least, reach a point at which the weakest of the four forces—the strong and weak nuclear forces, the electromagnetic force, and gravitational attraction—becomes strong enough to reverse direction from one of expansion to one of contraction. The Big Bang might be followed by an expansion followed by a contraction and a big crunch, after which another sequence can begin again.

John Wheeler (1977) has suggested that this 'reprocessing model' of cosmology might be probabilistic rather than deterministic. If every law that governs physical processes happens to be deterministic, then if the complete set of initial conditions remains constant across every reconstitution of the universe from one cycle to another, then the sequence of successive states of the universe should remain exactly the same from one cycle to another. If even one law that governs these processes happens to be probabilistic, however, then the sequence of successive states of the universe need not remain exactly the same from one cycle to another. The universe could attain one maximum volume and endure for one temporal interval during one cycle, but have another volume and duration in another cycle, and so forth—even under the same initial conditions!

More recent studies of the Big Bang model have been presented by Steven Weinberg (1977/88) and by Stephen Hawking (1988), who have also addressed themselves to the emergence of ultimate theories that would bring together the four forces within a single unified account (Ferguson 1991; Weinberg 1992). Big Bang models confront problems that continue to be explored today, such as whether there is enough mass in the universe to permit gravitational recycling (Wilford 1996a) and whether the universe might not peter out in a big whimper, after all (Wilford 1997). But even those who want to insist that the world had a beginning in time are apparently compelled to admit that—with qualifications of the kinds that I have acknowledged—the possibility that the world might have had no beginning and might have no end seems to be not only an abstract but also a physical possibility.

## 0.4  *Do Biology and Physics Conflict?*

The Steady State and the Big Bang models are far from the only theories that have been advanced to account for the origin of the universe from either historical (Munitz 1957) or contemporary perspectives (Lerner 1992). Eric J. Lerner, for example, suggests that Big Bang advocates are embracing a medieval conception according to which the universe was created from nothing and attained its greatest degree of perfection at—or even prior to—the moment of Creation. He maintains that there tends to be a striking correspondence between views dominant in cosmology and those dominant in society, where Big Bang models appear to be harmonious with doctrines of Christian theology. He even cites Pope Pius II, who relates the dissipation of energy during the history of the universe through increasing entropy to God's existence and a last judgment (Lerner 1992, p. 392).

While Lerner reports that some theologians view the existence of a finite universe—a universe with a definite beginning and a limited duration in time—as evidence of the subordination of the universe to God, our discussion of the Big Bang model indicates that the conclusion that the universe was created from nothing, *ex nihilo*, only arises if we reject the possibility that the universe may have had no beginning and no end. If the history of the universe is one of eternal recycling, perhaps the universe is not subordinate to God, after all. If all the laws of the universe are deterministic and the initial conditions remain the same from one cycle to another, it might make more sense to view the end of every cycle as merely a stage in the eternal recurrence than as the occasion for final judgment.

The notion that the universe attained its greatest perfection at—or even prior to—the moment of creation appears to be motivated by considerations revolving about entropy, which derive from the second law of thermodynamics. As Paul Davies has observed, in its widest sense, this law maintains that the universe as a whole becomes increasingly disordered, because the distribution of matter and energy tends away from states of greater heterogeneity toward states of greater homogeneity (Davies 1983, p. 10). If the second law of thermodynamics were a deterministic law having no exceptions and if "perfection" were properly defined as a state of minimum entropy, then perhaps the universe does attain its greatest state of perfection prior to the moment of creation, understood as the moment at which the Big Bang occurred. But such a view would be rather difficult to defend.

The second law of thermodynamics has both a narrow and a broad interpretation. In its narrow sense, it applies exclusively to systems that are closed, which means that no interaction with other systems takes place. Even under this interpretation, however, constancy in entropy is permissible with reversible systems (Feynman 1963, p. 44–12). Steady State and Big Bang recycling models are both compatible with the second law. In its broad sense, it assumes the standing of a statistical generalization depicting the average behavior of collections of systems (Rogers 1960, p. 395). To the extent to which the Creation of forms of life from non-life and new forms of life from old forms of life reflect decreasing entropy by systems that are open, biological evolution on a local scale is still compatible with entropy increases on a global scale. Evolution and entropy needn't conflict.

It would be a remarkable circumstance, of course, if the laws of biology could be true only if the laws of physics were false. It does not even seem obvious that science and religion necessarily stand in conflict. As

Michael Shermer has observed, conflicts with religion depend on rather specific beliefs, which are by no means universally shared (Shermer 2000, Chapter 6). Pope John Paul II, for example, has placed the authority of the Roman Catholic Church behind evolutionary theory with his decree that the Church supports the view that the human body may have been the product of a gradual process of evolution (Taliabue 1996; Applebome 1996). The human soul remains the province of God. Perhaps this should come as no surprise; after all, if God is omniscient and omnipotent, He could have utilized any method He preferred to create living things. Thus, if the laws of physics are incompatible with the laws of biology or if religion must conflict with science, we need to discover why.

# CHAPTER 1

# Why Does the Right
# Wage War on Darwin?

*• God's creation of the world and everything in it
can be reconciled with evolution; God's creation of
fixed species a few thousand years ago cannot be
reconciled with evolution*

*• Natural selection is one of at least eight causal
mechanisms of evolution: others are genetic
mutation, sexual reproduction, genetic drift,
sexual selection, group selection, artificial selection,
and genetic engineering*

*• Attempts to deny that there are biological laws are
misconceived*

*• Creation Science is not science because its claims are
not conditional, not testable, and not tentative*

*• When you talk to Creation Scientists, you find that
although they reject macro-evolution, they embrace
micro-evolution*

$T$he tension between science and religion has emerged in the form of an ongoing confrontation between evolution and Creationism as incompatible ways of looking at the world. The present religious challenge to evolution comes, not from the Roman Catholic Church, but from Protestant fundamentalism.

If Creationism is understood as the view that God created the world and everything therein, it is not incompatible with the scientific consensus. God may have chosen to create a world governed by laws of nature, including evolutionary processes. If Creationism is the view that God created every living thing in the form of species or 'kinds', whose properties are fixed and cannot change through time, then Creationism and evolution contradict each other: they cannot both be true.

There are important differences between distinct varieties of Creationism. In his book, *The Creationists*, ironically subtitled *The Evolution of Creationism*, Ronald L. Numbers distinguishes between three major movements: 'day-age theory', which interprets the seven days described in Genesis as seven epochs of long duration; 'the gap theory', which introduces a lengthy temporal separation between the creation of the world and a much later, seven-day creation of human beings; and 'Creation Science', as a contemporary movement which insists that Earth is less than ten thousand years old, that genetic variations are strictly limited, and that Earth has undergone a world-wide flood (Numbers 1992, pp. x–xi).

Proponents of Creation Science maintain that Creation Science is science and therefore ought to be taught along with evolution as part of the science curriculum in our public schools (Schmidt 1996). If Creationism as defined is incompatible with evolution this, of course, doesn't show that Creationism is not science nor that it should not be taught as part of the public-school science curriculum. Possibly Creation Science and evolution are merely two scientific alternatives equally deserving of inclusion.

In order to establish that Creationism is not science—if that, indeed, turns out to be the case—it's necessary not only to define 'Creationism' but also to define 'science' and then to demonstrate that science, as defined, excludes Creation Science. If 'Creationism' or 'science' were inadequately represented by the concepts employed for this purpose, it would be appropriate to object that the conclusion that Creation Science is not science has not be shown to be the case. Moreover, even if Creation Science were thereby shown to be non-science, this would not show that Creationism is non-sense nor would it show that evolution is science. Possibly, Creationism might not be science but might still make a lot of sense.

Science can be seen as pursuing the study of causes and effects, which are related by means of causal laws. From this perspective, the universe (all of creation) can be viewed as an *effect* that has been brought about by some *cause* (or Creator). That cause or Creator, in turn, however, might be natural or supernatural in character, where 'supernatural' causes exist or occur beyond the normal boundaries of human experience and cannot be explained by known forces or laws of nature (Webster 1988, p. 1344). To the extent to which 'Creationism' invokes or appeals to supernatural forces or causes, therefore, it cannot qualify as science, because the scope of science is confined to natural forces and causes.

**Figure 1.1** Science as the Study of Causes and Effects

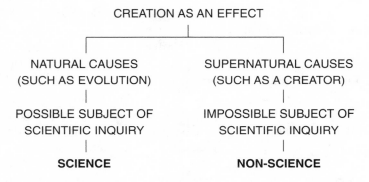

That this is indeed the case may be illustrated in a variety of different ways. Consider, for example, that space and time (space-time in relativity) can be represented by a series of squares, each of which represents a location at a time where the vertical columns may be taken to represent different locations and the horizontal rows different times at those locations, in order to achieve the effect of representing various locations at various times. Then, in relation to NOW, which stands for the present, events that occurred previously belong to the past, while those that will occur subsequently belong to the future—a distinction, of course, that is relative to the specific moment that is the NOW.

Causal connections thus obtain between space-time regions when the occurrence of an event at one such space-time region brings about an event at another space-time region, where the former stands to the latter as cause to effect. Ordinarily, these regions are assumed to be touching each other, both in space and in time, in the absence of 'action at a distance', which would involve the occurrence of an event at one region bringing about an event at another but non-contiguous region. Thus, if

**Figure 1.2** An Isolated Region of Local Space and Time

- t <················································ | ····················································> + t

PAST        NOW        FUTURE

we were to imagine lower-case letter assignments to locations and numerical assignments to times, then the occurrence of an event such as the striking of a match at *d3*, for example, might bring about the occurrence of an event such as the lighting of a match at *d4*, but not at *e7*. 'Action at a distance' can be accounted for on the basis of causal chains.

There are accounts of causation according to which 'causes' are nothing more than instances of properties that are regularly associated with instances of other properties in space and time. Thus, if every event of kind *striking of a match* in specific regions of space and time were to be followed by an event of kind *lighting of a match* at that same location immediately thereafter and if this pattern was displayed throughout space-time in the form of either a constant conjunction or stable relative frequency relating events of those kinds, then those regular assocations would qualify as 'natural laws'. Constant conjunctions of events of appropriate kinds in space-time would therefore imply the existence of corresponding deterministic laws, whereas stable relative frequencies of events of such kinds would imply the existence of probabilistic laws. They will be bona fide laws, however, only if they cannot be violated and cannot be changed (see the Appendix).

Causal hypotheses can be subjected to empirical test by conducting suitable observations, experiments, and measurements to ascertain whether the extensional distributions that would be most probable if the hypotheses are true in fact occur, a relationship represented by a *Causal Theory Square* (Fetzer 1993):

**Figure 1.3** A Causal Theory Square

Cause [C] is related by law to effect [E]

deductively              deductively
or                       or
inductively              inductively

Empirical test for [C] is correlated with empirical test for [E]

Thus, securing appropriate evidence to test causal hypotheses presupposes the possibility of detecting the presence or the absence of the occurrence of events of both kinds by observation, experimentation, or measurement. If the presence or absence of God as a possible cause (a 'supernatural' square) of the universe as an effect (the 'natural' squares) cannot be detected by empirical tests, then hypotheses of God as Creator would be unscientific.

# 1.1 *What Is Evolution?*

That the existence or non-existence of a God-as-Creator, when God is envisioned as a supernatural force that transcends the scope of human knowledge, cannot be established by reliance upon empirical procedures should come as no surprise. If God's presence or absence could be established on that basis, then discovering God's existence would be a subject for scientific research rather than a matter of religious faith. Perhaps even more striking, within the present context, is the realization that some effects—such as cancer as an effect of smoking—may take some time to become manifest, not in violation of the proscription against 'action at a distance' but because the effects of these causes are cumulative rather than immediate. A long sequence of events of the kind *smoking* (one string of squares) can bring about another sequence of the kind *cancer* (another string of squares) if they are related by causal chains.

Establishing that a long-term effect of the kind *cancer* is brought about by a long-term cause of the kind *smoking* thus appears more difficult than establishing that an immediate effect of the kind *lighting of a match* is brought about by a short-term cause of the kind *striking of a match*. The former, after all, tends to require most if not all of the developmental history of a human being before its effects become evident, whereas the latter becomes evident virtually immediately. Cigarette companies have long insisted that the connection between smoking and cancer was only one of correlation and not one of causation, a position that was abandoned only recently when one of the nation's major cigarette manufacturers acknowledged that cigarettes cause cancer (Broder 1997). This admission was the culmination of a protracted battle lasting many decades.

One reason this debate had been prolonged for so long is the difficulties encountered in establishing causal connections depending on prolonged exposure to causes in order to bring about their effects. Discovering the existence of complex patterns of causation over lengthy intervals of time requires extensive historical records, sophisticated statistical analyses, and investigations to exclude alternative explanations. Explanations for the occurrence of phenomena that involve causal chains that extend, not just over the history of development of individual organisms, but over histories of generation after generation of organisms through geological time, therefore, are going to be all the more difficult to discover. The pattern of inference, however, is the same.

The phenomena that alternative theories of evolution are intended to explain include the fossil record, geological strata, morphological similarities, DNA relations and the like, including the existence of about one and a half million living species whose existence has been identified and classified, a relatively small proportion of all species, which may number between ten and one hundred times that number (Wilson 1992, p. 134). Of the approximately one million animal species whose existence has been identified and classified, the vast majority are insects. Even though by far the greatest number of individual organisms inhabit land, it turns out that by far the greatest number of *kinds* of organisms or *phyla*, the highest level of biological classification below *kingdom*, inhabit the sea (Wilson 1992, p. 136).

In order to explain the fossil record, geological strata, morphological similarities, DNA relations, and so forth—the *evolutionary explanandum* as a description of the phenomena to be explained—most if not all tend to adopt the following three assumptions:

(A1)   More are born alive into each species than survive to reproduce.

(A2)   Many traits of organisms—whether plant or animal—are hereditary.

(A3)   Many traits of successive generations depend on those who survive.

**Figure 1.4** The Evolutionary Explanandum (Forey 1988)

# HISTORY OF THE EARTH

| EPOCH | SIGNIFICANT EVENTS | AGE |
|---|---|---|
| Recent | Ice retreats to present position | |
| Pleistocene (Ice Age) | Ice covers much of Europe and North America | |
| | | 2 |
| Pliocene | Climate becomes colder. Many mammals become extinct. Appearance of man | |
| | | 6 |
| Miocene | Rise and spread of grasslands, associated with spread of grazing mammals | |
| | | 22 |
| Oligocene | Many early mammals become extinct | |
| | | 36 |
| Eocene Paleocene | Early mammals diversify. Appearance of many modern mammal groups | |
| | | 65 |
| | Many animals become extinct, including dinosaurs and ammonites. Rise of flowering plants | |
| | | 145 |
| | Peak of dinosaur diversity. Rise of birds | |
| | | 210 |
| | Reptiles diversify rapidly. First mammals appear | |
| | | 250 |
| Pennsylvanian (Coal Age) | Widespread exinction of marine animals. Mammal-like reptiles diversify | |
| | | 290 |
| Mississipian | Coal swamps with lush vegetation. Rise of winged insects and primitive reptiles | |
| | | 340 |
| | Widespread shallow seas with reefs. Amphibians diversify | |
| | | 365 |
| | Widespread invasion of fresh water by animals and plants. Rise of ammonoids in sea. Fishes diversify | |
| | | 415 |
| | Rise of land plants. Prolific life in shallow seas | |
| | | 465 |
| | Spread of shallow seas over land. Marine invertebrates diversify rapidly | |
| | | 510 |
| | Many animals develop hard skeletons | |
| | | 575 |
| | Soft bodied animals and algae present, including stromatolites | |
| | Development of free oxygen | 3000 |
| | Birth of planet Earth | 4600 |

| SYSTEM | PERIOD | LIFE FORMS |
|---|---|---|
| Cenozoic | Quaternary | |
| | Tertiary | |
| Mesozoic (Age of Dinosaurs) | Cretaceous | |
| | Jurrasic | |
| | Triassic | |
| Paleozoic | Permian | |
| | Carboniferous | |
| | Devonian (Age of Fishes) | |
| | Silurian | |
| | Ordovician | |
| | Cambrian (Trilobytes) | |
| Precambrian | | |

The first of these, (A1), is usually attributed to Thomas Robert Malthus (1766–1834), an English economist; the second, (A2), to Gregor Mendel (1822–84), an Austrian monk; the third, (A3), to Charles Darwin (1809–82), an English naturalist.

Although (A3) might seem to be an obvious consequence of (A1) and (A2) when presented as it has been here—where it could even be characterized as a theorem following from (A1) and (A2) as axioms and reformulated to say, *Many traits of successive generations* thus *depend upon those who survive*—Darwin was unaware of Mendel's findings, which laid the foundation for genetics. While he was aware of Malthus's research, therefore, Darwin was not in the position to derive (A3) from (A1) and (A2), but worked very hard to establish its truth on independent grounds, especially through observations and measurements that he conducted during five years as a naturalist aboard *H.M.S. Beagle* during its 1831–36 voyage around the world (Browne 1995). Consequently, the merging of these three theses is called 'the modern synthesis' or 'neo-Darwinism'.

The most famous of Darwin's contributions concerns the role of competition between the members of one species ('conspecifics') for food, shelter, and other limited resources—including especially sexual mates, without whom sexual reproduction is impossible. (At least, until recently among humans, when sperm banks and artificial insemination became possible, though this method of reproduction, unlike cloning, continues to require a genetic contribution from a member of each sex.) Thus, those who possess competitive advantages are more likely to reproduce. Since those who reproduce are among those who survive, Darwin's observation has come to be known as 'the survival of the fittest', even though that may or may not be an accurate depiction, a matter to which we shall turn in Chapter 2.

Darwin referred to competition between conspecifics as 'natural selection', suggesting that it was among the most, if not *the* most, important causal mechanisms that contribute to evolution. The special causal factors that determine which bodies and brains, known as 'phenotypes', are perpetuated from generation to generation, moreover, are known as 'genotypes' consisting of complete sets of genes for *individual organisms*. This notion may be distinguished from that of the 'genome' as the complete set of genes for *human beings*, whether male or female, African or Oriental, and so forth (Schuler *et al.* 1996). Among biologists, evolution is measured by changes in gene pools across time.

Conclusions about the existence of genes and the traits they influence—individually or in combination—are derived here, as in other sciences, on the basis of *inference to the best explanation*. Consideration must be given to the available hypotheses and theories that might possibly explain the evidence or the phenomena. A simple example might consist of evidence that poodles beget poodles, that Chinese beget Chinese, and so on. The hypotheses might include that this is a *chance* phenomenon (that sometimes poodles beget Chinese and sometimes Chinese beget poodles, more or less on a random basis), that it is a *probabilistic* phenomenon (that there is a constant probability for poodles to beget poodles and to beget Chineses, a constant probability for Chinese to beget Chineses and to beget poodles), or that it is a *deterministic* phenomenon (where poodles only beget poodles, Chinese only beget Chinese, and so forth), where inference to the best explanation supports the deterministic alternative.

Although it has become common practice to refer to 'evolution' and to 'natural selection' as though they were synonymous, *natural selection* in Darwin's sense is only one among at least eight different causal mechanisms, which contribute to evolution as it is measured by changes in gene pools across time, including genetic mutation, natural selection, sexual reproduction, genetic drift, sexual selection, group selection, artificial selection, and genetic engineering. Four of these—genetic mutation, sexual reproduction, genetic drift, and genetic engineering—are sources of genetic variation within gene pools, while the other four—natural selection, sexual selection, group selection, and artificial selection—are mechanisms that determine which genes happen to be perpetuated from earlier gene pools to later gene pools (Williams 1966).

The distinction between causal mechanisms that contribute to evolution and the means by which it is measured has sometimes been described as the difference between the *levels* of selection and the *units* of selection (Sober 1984). The units of selection are supposed to be what is selected—that is, what is perpetuated—during evolution, which would appear to be individual genes as the transmissible entities that give rise to heritable traits. (Genotypes and phenotypes cannot be the units of selection, because—absent cloning—they are not perpetuated in subsequent gene pools.) The level of selection thus becomes the kinds of causal mechanisms that contribute to determining which genes are and which are not perpetuated in subsequent gene pools. While it may seem plausible to suppose that selection usually operates at the level of the phenotype, we shall discover reasons for doubting that this is generally true.

A few illustrations of some of these mechanisms may be appropriate here, though others will be exemplified elsewhere. *Genetic mutation*, for example, occurs when genes of one kind are transformed into genes of another kind, a phenomenon that can occur with no significant effects.

Matt Ridley estimates that there are as many as one hundred mutations per genotype in mammals: "That is, your children will have one hundred differences from you and your spouse in their genes as a result of random copying errors by your enzymes or as a result of mutations in your ovaries or testicles caused by cosmic rays" (Ridley 1993, p. 45). These represent a rather small percentage of (what are called) 'point' mutations, where, with about seventy-five million points per genotype, one hundred point mutations may occur, of which perhaps as much as ninety-two percent have no phenotypic effects.

The importance of genetic mutation, however, becomes quite apparent in view of the multiple differences that (relatively limited) genetic changes can make due to the influence of polygenic interactions and pleiotropic effects (see Lennox 1992). *Polygenic interactions* take place when more than one pair of genes interact to produce specific phenotypic traits, while *pleiotropic effects* occur when single pairs of genes produce multiple differences in phenotypes. An especially striking example of the importance of these causal mechanisms occurs in comparisons between human beings and chimpanzees, to whom we are closely related. Estimates suggest we share more than ninety-eight percent of our chromosomes, yet our differences—including our behavior—are quite extensive, which emphasizes the importance of that two-percent difference (Lumsden and Wilson 1983).

A striking and disturbing example of natural selection has been observed in relation to the evolution of bacteria resistant to the antibiotics used by medical doctors to combat infections. Many patients stop taking their medicine when they start to feel better, even though prescriptions specify completing the treatment by taking every dose prescribed. The result has been that weaker bacteria tend to be extinguished by penicillin, for example, but that the remaining bacteria, which are the most resistant to extinction, survive and reproduce, generating stronger, more penicillin-resistant, species (Garrett 1995). Recent outbreaks of food poisoning in Japan and around the world have been traced to *E. coli* bacteria that have acquired a gene for production of shiga toxin (Hilts 1996).

Another less-disturbing example of natural selection has emerged from recent studies of aquatic life in Lake Victoria, the largest lake in Africa. The age of the lake, which used to be a dry, grassy plain, has now been measured by means of carbon-14 dating, and turns out be about twelve thousand years. Over three-hundred species of cichlid fish inhabit these waters, all descended from one ancestral population, showing amazingly rapid emergence of new species in a comparatively short time

(Johnson 1996). Evolutionary theorists were surprised by the discovery of such rapid evolution (Yoon 1996).

In later chapters we're going to consider examples of genetic drift, group selection, and genetic engineering as well as additional illustrations of natural selection. The primary benefit of *sexual reproduction* seems to be an increase in genetic diversity that occurs when offspring possess half of their genes from each of their parents (Margulis and Sagan 1986). Precisely which conspecifics tend to mate and reproduce, however, is strongly affected by *sexual selection* on the basis of traits that members of the opposite sex tend to find attractive, which can take a fascinating variety of forms (Gould and Gould 1996). Sometimes nature is not allowed to have its way, however, due to the intrusion of *artificial selection* by parents on behalf of their children (arranged marriages) or by breeders on behalf of their profits (selective breeding), whose purpose is to leave as little to chance as possible in regard to reproduction (Michod 1995).

In a broader sense, the phrase 'natural selection' tends to be treated as encompassing every mode or mechanism that contributes to the evolution of species, including all the above. The theory of evolution as a set of causal mechanisms that might be invoked to explain the explanandum of the fossil record (geological strata, morphological similarities, and so forth) is less a single defined entity than it is a family of theories consisting of different combinations of causal mechanisms, where each theory consists of a set of laws that apply to a common domain. Consider the following alternatives:

(**EH-1**)　Life has evolved by means of genetic mutation;

(**EH-2**)　Life has evolved by that plus natural selection;

(**EH-3**)　Life has evolved by that plus sexual reproduction;

(**EH-4**)　Life has evolved by that plus genetic drift;

(**EH-5**)　Life has evolved by that plus sexual selection;

(**EH-6**)　Life has evolved by that plus group selection;

(**EH-7**)　Life has evolved by that plus artificial selection;

(**EH-8**)　Life has evolved by that plus genetic engineering.

Each of these is successively stronger in adding one more causal mechanism to the sets of causal mechanisms posited by previous alternatives. The 'theory of evolution' consists of families of theories that are not exhausted by these alternatives, since additional hypotheses such as the inheritance of acquired characteristics or other possible mechanisms are available, at least some of which have been taken seriously (Richards 1987).

From the perspective of inference to the best explanation, therefore, the question arises, not whether evolutionary hypotheses (EH-1) to (EH-8) are true, but whether they qualify as possible explanations for the evidence *e*:

**Figure 1.5** Alternative Evolutionary Theories

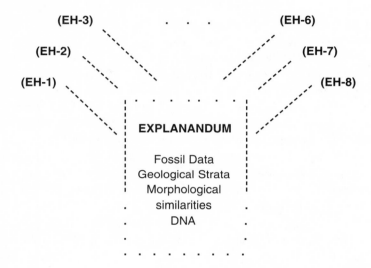

where the best theory will confer the highest nomic expectability upon the explanandum and thereby achieve the highest degree of explanatory power while adopting the fewest explanatory principles to create an elegant theory. In other words the best explanation will be the one that confers the highest probability upon the explanandum, relative to its explanatory premises, which include laws and initial conditions (see the Appendix).

Perhaps the most striking difference between the classic Creationist hypotheses we have considered and these evolutionary hypotheses is that there appears to be scant room for doubt about the *explanatory potential* of these evolutionary hypotheses. Each of these causal mechanisms—genetic mutation, natural selection, sexual reproduction, genetic drift, sexual selection, group selection, artificial selection, and genetic engineering—is *implicitly lawful*. Genetic mutation, for example, presupposes the existence of the potential for mutation as a permanent property of genes, whereby specific changes in their types are (invariably or probably) brought about as effects of specific causes, such as exposure to specific environments.

Similar considerations apply to natural selection, sexual reproduction, and every other member of this list, where the only debatable exception is group selection, which has been subject to intense criticism by those committed to individual selection (Williams 1966; 1992). Reasons some people have given for denying the existence of laws of biology thus appear to be bad ones, rooted in misunderstandings of the differences between properties and classes and the logical character of laws themselves, which need not have any instances at all (see the Appendix).

Most of the objections raised against evolutionary hypotheses have to do with questions about *initial conditions*, such as whether or not theories of the origin of the universe and of the origin of Earth provide enough time for evolution thus understood to produce the number or diversity of species found today. It is believed that Earth came into existence around five billion years ago, that animal life began about six hundred million years ago, and that hominid life emerged around five million years ago (Asimov 1987). The prospect that intelligent life has evolved elsewhere in the universe, however, increases with each astronomical study (Wilford 1996b). And the latest reports suggest that the first micro-organisms—initially lacking even nucleuses—may even have emerged as long as 3.5 to 4 billion years ago (Wilford 1996c).

Nevertheless, the most serious of objections that have recently been raised about the capacity of evolution to account for the evolution of species have concerned the very idea of species itself. Past practice has been to define sexually reproducing 'species' employing biological criteria for reproductive behavior:

> **species** = *df* a population whose members tend to interbreed freely under natural conditions (Wilson 1992, p. 38)

where the origin of species is simply the emergence of some difference—any difference at all—that inhibits the production of fertile hybrids between the members of populations under natural conditions (Wilson 1992, p. 56). Thus, the differences between species tend to originate as traits that adapt members to the environment rather than as devices for reproductive isolation (Wilson 1992, p. 59). The objection that has been raised to this conception has come both from biologists and philosophers, who have offered an alternative view.

## 1.2  *Are Species Individuals?*

The thesis advocated by the philosopher David Hull (1978) and the biologists Ernst Mayr (1988) and Michael Ghiselin (1997) is that species are not classes but individuals, a distinction that makes an enormous theoretical difference to major issues in evolutionary theory. This thesis threatens the account of evolution that I am presenting to the extent to which it tends to undermine the plausibility of the conception of laws of biology and especially of evolution; for, if species are individuals, while laws concern entities of some other kind, then there are no laws of biology.

It may seem ironic that philosophers of the science of biology should maintain that there are no laws of biology, which in turn implies that biology is not a science, but that is how things are. In my view their arguments are based upon misconceptions.

To forestall misunderstanding, it should be observed that the term 'individual' occurs in biological contexts with a variety of meanings. Sometimes it just means 'organism', but sometimes it has a more generic sense, where, for example, genes are individuals, hearts are individuals, and beehives are individuals. When a biologist describes a gene as an individual, he certainly does not mean that this gene is an organism. The matter is about the nature of the entities that can occur as objects of quantification in lawlike sentences, that is, the entities over which the variable '$x$' ranges in sentences of the kinds discussed in the Appendix. It shouldn't be surprising, therefore, to discover that this issue may hinge on rather precise and technical distinctions.

Several distinctions must be introduced between intensions and extensions, classes and members, and classes and properties. Speaking generally, common nouns such as 'marble', 'chair', 'unicorn', have both intensions and extensions. Their *intensions* are specified by the conditions that must be satisfied for something to be properly described by that word; their *extensions* consist of everything there is that satisfies those conditions. The term 'marble', for example, might be defined as a little ball of stone, glass or clay used in games; or, alternatively, it can be defined as a hard, crystalline or granular, metamorphic limestone, white or variously colored and sometimes streaked or mottled, which can take a high polish and is much used in building and sculpture (Webster 1988).

Under the first such definition, the intension of the term 'marble' is a little ball of stone, glass, or clay used in games, and the extension of the term is everything there is that satisfies those conditions, namely: every instance of those conditions—past, present, or future—or, in other words, the complete set of marbles. Under the second definition given, the intension of the term 'marble' is hard, crystalline or granular, metamorphic limestone, while the extension of the term is everything there is that satisfies those conditions, namely: every instance of those conditions—past, present, or future—or every chunk, block, piece or chip or whatever that instantiates that kind of material.

These alternative definitions of 'marble' exemplify two different kinds of common nouns, which Quine has referred to as 'count nouns' and 'mass nouns' (Quine 1960). *Count nouns* describe things that come 'prepackaged' and that can be counted; thus, a certain collection of marbles (in the first sense) might have five or ten marbles as its members, and other collections might have more or less. *Mass nouns*, however, describe things that do not come 'prepackaged', which must therefore be measured quantitatively by other means. Things that are (made of) marble might be statues, buildings, blocks, chips, or whatever, where as *statues of* marble, as *buildings of* marble, as marble *blocks* or marble *chips* they might be counted (as number of instances of things of that marble kind), but where 'how much' marble as such might require other units of measure: by weight (in tonnage), by volume (in cubic meters), or whatever.

In relation to the extension of 'marble' in the first sense, there is a natural unit of measurement when it comes to quantitative considerations, how many? In relation to the extension of 'marble' in the second sense, however, the natural unit of measurement is not, how many?, but rather, how much? This difference might be said to reflect the consideration that 'marble' in the second sense is a kind of material out of which things of many different kinds might be made, while 'marble' in the first sense is a kind of thing that can be made of many different kinds of material. Notice, too, that 'marble' in the second sense is defined as '*a* hard, crystalline or granular, metamorphic limestone, white or variously colored', as *a kind—or one kind—of limestone*, where there may also be various other kinds. As a kind of limestone, marble might also qualify as one of four or five kinds of limestone, where even (initially) mass nouns may describe countable phenomena at some level of description.

The instances of intensions of common nouns such as 'marble', 'chair', and 'unicorn' are also known as 'members' of their extensions, where these collections of members satisfying the same intensions are also known as 'classes'. Classes, however, are generally assumed to be entirely extensional entities, in the sense that two classes are the same, necessarily, if their members are the same, which is not assumed to be the case for intensions. To distinguish between the classes of things that satisfy specific conditions and the specific conditions they satisfy, therefore, a distinction is ordinarily drawn between *classes* and *properties*. As outlined in the Appendix, Quine (1951) has explained that classes can be treated as properties if the notion of property is qualified and properties become identical when their instances are identical.

Just because a position can be taken does not imply that it ought to be. We already know that this move, which separates nominalists from realists, has the consequence that being a unicorn, being a vampire, and being a werewolf are one and the same property. Indeed, they are now simply three words for naming the same property, because properties must be the same when their instances are the same. The same holds for classes that have members. In a world in which it happens that all and only oval lockets are made of gold, for example, the phrases (thing that is an) 'oval locket' and (thing that is) 'made of gold', where the first is a count noun and the second not, would apply to all and only the same things, yet we should not be tempted to suppose there is or would be no difference between those properties for that reason (Fetzer 1981).

These reflections suggest that nominalism is a peculiar and rather difficult doctrine to defend, notwithstanding the ingenuity some may display in its defense. But the same considerations suggest there exists a fundamental difference between *classes* (as extensional entities) and *properties* (as intensional entities) that strongly affects the plausibility of the species are individuals thesis. For it appears evident that these authors may have overlooked a third alternative, namely: that species are properties, at least insofar as the term 'species' has both an intension and an extension, where that extension is not null but encompasses everything that satisfies its intension as members of the corresponding class. But this is a case where membership in the class is determined not by arbitrary congregation—as in the case of an old comb, the square root of −1, and the current President of the United States—but by some corresponding property.

Hull and others employ the term 'class' in an ambiguous fashion and when levels of description are considered it is not difficult to infer that what they really mean is synonymous with (or, at least, close to) the meaning of 'property' as an intensional notion. Suppose we assume that their basic claim is correct, namely: that things that are individuals are not classes and that things that are classes are not individuals, as though that could be determined independently of some specific presupposed level of description. Then the problem becomes, what happens to the *members* of a species? Presumably they are individuals or they are classes, by hypothesis. But if they are individuals, then either they are members of another—higher order—individual or they are members of a class. And if they are members of another—higher order—individual, then what sense does it make to characterize that entity as an individual rather than as a class?

*Species as natural kinds*, *species as properties*, and *species as classes* are, at the very least, the kinds of things that can have members, but what sense does it make to adopt the theory that *species as individuals* neverthe-less have members? There are cases in which it makes sense to say that something is composed of other things, where those other things are parts of that something and where that something qualifies as an individual. Organisms, for example, consist of (instances of) arrangements of cells, which are parts of arrangements of molecules, of organs (heart, kidney, liver, and so forth) and of structures (muscular, skeletal, nervous, and the like). Those cells, organs and structures are all parts of an organism as components of a larger system. It could be said of them taken altogether that they are members of a class. And it could be said of them that they are members of a class that consists of parts of an organism.

Perhaps it could also be said of them that they are members of a class consisting of the parts of a single—or individual—organism. But it would be wrong to say of those cells, those organs, or those structures that they were not themselves single—or individual—cells, organs or structures. So individual cells, individual organs and individual structures can be parts of individual organisms. We can even count them! Indeed, if we want a 'rule of thumb' to tell whether we are dealing with individuals, then try counting them. If we are able to say how many there are, then we have succeeded in treating them as individuals.

If we were to take a single, individual organism and ask, how many?, *in the absence of any specification of the kind of thing we were taking about,* the answer would be indeterminate: there might be one organism and one heart, but two kidneys, many organs, lots of bones, huge numbers of cells, and so forth. Without specifying the kinds of things we are talking about, there is no determinate answer to the question, how many? The question has a determinate answer only on the assumption that we have specified or presupposed *the kinds of things* we have in mind relative to which there will be so many *things that are of that kind* in a given case. With respect to mass nouns, such as 'blood', moreover, we must specify the unit of meas-urement in liters, milliliters, or some other measure.

Unfortunately, this result is perfectly general, which means that whether something is or is not an individual is relative to a certain level of description. Traditional biological classifications reflect a (roughly, hierarchical) sequence of successive more and more general properties distinguishing between different kinds of things. These properties repre-sent abstractions in relation to those below them, where the sequence from species to genus to family to order to class to phylum to kingdom reflects a progression from larger and more detailed arrangements of properties to successive smaller and less detailed arrangements of proper-ties. *Even at the highest level, however, there are individuals*—in this case, individual kingdoms, which can be enumerated and counted: viral, bacterial, fungal, plant and animal, respectively—just as there are individual phyla, classes, orders, families, genera and species. Viewed intensionally as classes that are defined by intensional membership properties, each of these categories contributes whatever it contributes to systematic understanding of the nature of biological organisms; but there are individuals at each level described.

From a logical point of view, the matter is elementary. The notion of a *sentential function* is defined by a (monadic, dyadic, or other) predicate that can be turned into a sentence that may be true or false four different ways, namely:

$$\_\_\_ \text{ is (an) } F$$

may be turned into a sentence by (a) filling in the blank by a proper name, (b) filling in the blank by an ambiguous name, (c) replacing the blank by a variable and binding that variable with a corresponding existential quantifier, or (d) replacing the blank by a variable and binding that variable with a corresponding universal quantifier. Then the list of proper names and ambiguous names that are possible values of the quantifiers thereby become the singular entities—or 'individuals'—within that system of notation (see Gustafson and Ulrich 1973).

The property under consideration, therefore, could be that something __ is made of gold or __ is an atom of polonium$^{218}$, which might be represented by $G$ __ or by $P^{218}$; __ , respectively, where instead of '__'s, logicians make use of '$x$'. Thus, '$Gx$' and '$P^{218}\ x$' are examples of sentential functions that maintain '$x$ is $G$' and '$x$ is $P^{218}$', respectively, which are the forms of possible sentences that are neither true nor false but which can be turned into sentences in four different ways. Replacing '$x$' with a proper name, such as '$c$' for Bill Clinton, '$Gx$' becomes '$Gc$', which asserts, 'Bill Clinton is (made of) gold'. Alternatively, replacing '$x$' with an ambiguous name, such as '$d$' for John Doe, '$Gx$' becomes '$Gd$', which asserts, 'John Doe is (made of) gold'. The use of the so-called existential quantifier, '$(Ex)$', can be prefixed to '$Gx$' to become, '$(Ex)Gx$', which asserts 'Something is (made of) gold', while the universal quantifier, '$x$', can be prefixed to '$Gx$' to become '$(x)Gx$', which asserts, 'Everything is (made of) gold'.

If the system includes names of kingdoms, for example, and '$F$' is replaced by a description of properties that kingdoms might possess—such as being populated by many phyla or by few phyla, then it could produce sentences such as, 'The viral kingdom has many phyla', 'Some kingdoms have few phyla', or 'Every kingdom has at least one phylum', and such, where the values of those variables are the individuals of that system. (Indeed, proper names are also known as 'individual constants' for this reason.) Thus, as I asserted above, *something qualifies as an individual relative to a certain level of description*, where things, such as species, could be individuals in relation to some levels of description relative to sentence functions that correspond to the range of predicates that describe properties that such a species may or may not have (ranging over every question that might be asked about them) but not others.

If organisms are the only kind of entity that is said to develop, for example, while species are said to evolve, then questions about the development of species or about the evolution of organisms are, strictly speaking, not well-formed and commit what is commonly referred to as a 'category mistake'. It would be logically improper, for example, to ask if David Hull, Michael Ghiselin, and Ernst Mayr had 'evolved'—which can be represented formally by employing corresponding sentence functions having names for them as individual constants—claims that would be regarded by convention as either false or meaningless. As it happens, this thesis appears to apply to everything, which means that, from a logical point of view, it is turns out to be mistaken and misleading to take species as individuals, even though the reasons are subtle and complex.

Now there is a legitimate question of whether it is more illuminating or not to consider *the history of evolution* that brings a species into existence as a defining property of that species, where the members of no other group—no matter how similar in their structure and function they may be: even if they are genetically, phenotypically, and behaviorally identical—should be classified as *members of the same species*. That is an interesting problem about the nature of biological classification and its theoretical objectives. But it does not require the drastic and unjustifiable conception of species as individuals for its solution. Indeed, it depends upon the construction of species as properties, intensionally understood, where one of those properties concerns the evolutionary origin or lineage of those who currently instantiate these properties. If this is the real issue, as I suspect, then perhaps this discussion may contribute to the debate.

The thesis that species are individuals appears to have been motivated, at least in part, by the belief that generalizations must have many instances and otherwise cannot qualify as laws. This is false, as I explain in the Appendix, because laws concern relations between properties, including causal mechanisms, which might or might not be instantiated during the world's history. Laws characterize permanent properties and their causal manifestations, where every causal mechanism, including those considered above, has implicitly lawful standing with respect to the conditions of its application and the effects it brings about. The reason most laws that have been discovered have many instances is that it can be difficult to discover laws when they have few or no actual instances.

Moreover, laws apply to things as instances of those reference properties and not as those individual things. A person of 200 lbs. weight, for example, is an instance of things having a certain mass in a fixed-strength gravitational field, of course, but also has other properties because he is an instance of the species *Homo sapiens*, including specific reproductive capacities, learning tendencies, and other properties as specific lawful manifestations of phenotypes developed of specific genotypes. These laws apply to instances of such reference properties regardless of whether they have been instantiated in the past.

And so those who hold there are laws for classes but not for individuals are wrong on both counts, because there are laws for individuals as instantiations of reference properties, but there are no laws for any extensional classes. The permanent property relationship, like the maximal specificity requirement, is so strong that it logically guarantees that the truth of any singular subjunctive conditional of the form, '$Rxt ==> Axt$', deductively implies the truth of the corresponding generalization, '$(x)(t)(Rxt ==> Axt)$', no matter whether it happens to be instantiated by an individual constant $c$, an ambiguous name $d$, or actually has no instances during the history of the world (Fetzer 1981, pp. 53–54).

The objections that Hull, Ghiselin, and Mayr raise to *essentialism*, a doctrine that takes species to have 'essences' that are immutable and can never change which emerge intermittently with great force, are at least partly rooted in their belief that essentialists would oppose their historical-evolutionary relativization of the species concept, which is no doubt correct. There are many reasons to object to essentialism, which Popper (1968), especially has raised, including, for example, that scientists have no way of discovering if essences do or do not exist.

## 1.3  *Is Creation Science Science?*

These considerations suggest that the thesis that species are individuals cannot be correct and therefore does not undermine the traditional biological conception of sexually reproducing species as populations whose members tend to interbreed freely under natural conditions (Wilson 1992). This is both a genetic and a behavioral definition, which might perhaps be improved upon by some heretofore overlooked alternative definition. The crucial consideration remains that science attempts to maximize the empirical content of its theories by whenever possible displacing 'analytical truths' relating properties (which are true by definition) by 'empirical truths' relating properties (which are not true by definition) through the adoption of reference properties in relation to which their instances have the maximal class of permanent properties (Fetzer 1981).

As Numbers (1992) observes, Creation Science has emerged as the most recent version of Creationism, one that claims to have the status of a science and that therefore should be included in the science curriculum of the public schools. The version we shall consider, which has been formulated by the Creation Scientist, Walter Brown (1995, p. 172), offers three theses about the history of the world:

(CS-1) Everything in the universe, including the stars, the solar system, the Earth, life, and man, came into existence suddenly and recently, in essentially the complexity that we see today;

(CS-2) Genetic variations are limited; and,

(CS-3) The earth has experienced a worldwide flood.

There is an ordinary sense of the term 'theory' in which something qualifies as a theory when it consists of any mere speculation, conjecture or guess. No doubt, Creation Science qualifies as a 'theory' in this sense, simply because it advances at least three speculations, conjectures, or guesses about the history of the world. The interesting question is not whether it qualifies as a 'theory' in this ordinary sense but whether it qualifies as a theory in the scientific sense, where a 'theory' must be a potentially explanatory lawlike hypothesis.

Activities that are called 'science', such as Library Science, Military Science, and Mortuary Science are not *therefore* sciences, because—in this case—they do not aim at the discovery of natural laws. Moreover, activities that are sciences are not always called by that name: physics, chemistry, and biology, for example, are sciences, even when they are not being called 'sciences'. The question that arises with respect to Creation Science, therefore, is not the trivial question of whether it is called 'science'—obviously, it is—but the non-trivial question of whether or not it actually is one. Sciences are distinguished by their aims and their methods, where physics aims at the discovery of laws of physics, chemistry of laws of chemistry, and so forth, by employing such methods as observation, experimentation, and inference to the best explanation.

Scientific knowledge assumes forms that are *conditional, testable,* and *tentative.* The conditionality of scientific hypotheses and theories arises from characterizing what properties or events will occur in the world as permanent properties or causal effects of the presence of other properties or the occurrence of other events. Such knowledge has to be testable, where it must be possible to detect the presence or absence of reference properties or events-as-causes and to detect the presence or absence of attribute properties or events-as-effects in order to subject those hypotheses and theories to empirical test. Moreover, scientific knowledge is tentative insofar as it is always subject to revision due to technological innovations, the acquisition of additional evidence, or the discovery of alternative hypotheses.

These conditions—of conditionality, testability, and tentativeness—supply a third approach to evaluating the scientific status of hypotheses and theories. The first, involving inference to the best explanation (described in the Appendix), shows that classic Creationist hypotheses are not scientific, because they cannot satisfy conditions of adequacy that are required to qualify as possible explanations for the explanandum phenomenon. The second, which we looked at earlier in this chapter, explains why appeals to supernatural causes cannot qualify as scientific, when scientific inquiries are confined to natural causes. The third, which we are now considering, bears strong affinities to the second, and, like the second, seems to be simpler and easier to apply than are appeals to inference to the best explanation.

If Creation Science is science, then it should satisfy the aim of science—the search for laws of nature—and the methodological desiderata characteristic of sciences—conditionality, testability, and tentativeness. Let us therefore apply this standard to the three Creation Science hypotheses, beginning with (CS-1). Thus, the first problem with hypothesis (CS-1) is that it appears to be *unconditional*: it does not specify the conditions under which events of the kinds that it describes would be expected to take place. These events were either caused or they were uncaused. If they were uncaused, then they are beyond scientific investigation. If they were caused, then their causes must be supernatural or natural. If they are supernatural, however, then they are beyond scientific investigation. If natural, those causes have to be specified to qualify as scientific.

Hypothesis (CS-1) also appears to be *untestable*. Neither the time of creation nor the degree of complexity to be found in the world 'today' is specified. It is therefore compatible with any time of creation or with any degree of complexity. Some classic philosophical examples of hypotheses of this kind include that the world was created five minutes ago, ten minutes ago, or an hour ago, but with exactly the properties we find present in the world today, including records of fossils, geological strata, and so on, even including our present memories with exactly the contents that they possess today. Another is the thesis of solipsism, namely: you think you exist in the world, but actually you are merely living a dream, because the world is nothing but a fabrication constructed by your mind. These are hypotheses that seem to be completely inaccessible to empirical test.

Hypothesis (CS-1) also seems to be *arbitrary*. It does not tell us, for example, whether the stars, the solar system, the earth, life, and man were the products of one act of creation or of many acts of creation. Indeed, it does not even tell us whether the one-or-more acts of creation were performed by one-or-more creators. It may sound odd because our Judeo-Christian culture has conditioned us to presuppose the existence of a single omniscient and omnipotent God. But surely there could be many gods, who specialize in various kinds of creative acts, some for viruses, some for bacteria, some for fungi, and so on. There appear to be no possible scientific answers to questions such as these. Everything that occurs, no matter what, could be claimed to be of supernatural origin.

This may be part of the humor found in the comedy routines of Flip Wilson, who—whenever he was caught doing something he should not have been doing, which was often—would proclaim, 'The Devil made me do it!' Events whose occurrence is supposed to contravene or violate natural laws are supposed to be 'miracles'. Scientists tend to take a dim view of allegations of miraculous occurrences. One of the most famous arguments against miracles was advanced by the Scottish philosopher, David Hume (1711–76), who observed that the evidence supporting the existence of laws of nature counts against the occurrence of miracles: in order to accept the accounts of those who claim that they have occurred, it has to be more improbable that those who claim to have witnessed miracles are mistaken than it is improbable that the laws of nature have been violated.

Moreover, this arbitrary, unconditional and untestable hypothesis seems to be held, not tentatively, but absolutely, come what may. If those who advance (CS-1) want to defend their acceptance as *tentative*, then they ought to explain under what circumstances they would be willing to surrender it as no longer tenable. A typical indication that a thesis is being held as an article of faith rather than as a rational belief derives from its apparent compatibility with any imaginable evidence. We have already seen that what would count as 'evidence' for or against such a hypothesis is not at all apparent. And even if there were circumstances under which someone who holds this hypothesis might be willing to give it up, those could not be scientific circumstances. An abritrary, unconditional, and untestable hypothesis is unscientific.

Hypothesis (CS-2), which holds that genetic variations are limited, suffers from other deficiencies. The extent to which genetic variation is supposed to be limited is not specified. Thus, so long as genetic variation is not unlimited (or infinite), this hypothesis is true. But there is an ambiguity. Under INTERPRETATION 1, genetic variations are limited insofar as *future* genetic variations are strictly limited to genes in existing gene pools. This interpretation, however, is incompatible with the occurrence of genetic mutations, for example, and therefore appears to be false. According to INTERPRETATION 2, by contrast, genetic variations are limited insofar as *present* genetic variations are strictly limited to genes in existing gene pools, which is true but trivial.

There is yet another alternative, INTERPRETATION 3, according to which genetic variations are strictly limited to evolution within species (let us call this 'microevolution') and does not extend to evolution between species (let us call this 'macroevolution'). Thus, creation scientists such as Brown (1995, p. 3) consider microevolution to be permissible but macroevolution not to be:

**(DE-1)  microevolution** = df a [naturally occurring] change that produces only minor chemical alterations or changes in size, shape or color that do not involve increasing complexity. (Sometimes called 'horizontal'.)

**(DE-2)  macroevolution** = df a naturally occurring, beneficial change that produces increasing and heritable complexity, which would be shown if the offspring of one form of life had a different and improved set of vital organs. (Sometimes called 'vertical'.)

Brown asserts that microevolution plus time will not produce macroevolution, while acknowledging that, 'Both Creationists and evolutionists agree that microevolution occurs' (Brown 1995, p. 3). Since evolution is measured in terms of changes in gene pools across time and microevolution involves changes in gene pools across time, microevolution is a form of evolution. Moreover, affirming the occurrence of microevolution while denying the occurrence of macroevolution is no more than *begging the question* by taking for granted what is at issue, namely: whether or not macroevolution as a natural phenomenon occurs.

Brown is right when he claims that such a distinction is drawn not only by creation scientists but by evolutionary biologists. Ricki Lewis, for example, in her biology text, *Life*, has defined these terms as follows (Lewis 1995, p. 398):

(DE-3) **microevolution** = *df* small-scale evolutionary events, including changes in individual allele (gene variant) frequencies within a population; and,

(DE-4) **macroevolution** = *df* large-scale evolutionary events, including the appearance of new species (speciation) and the disappearance of species (extinction).

Anyone who engages in public debate with Creation Scientists, as I have done, soon discovers that the debate is not between 'evolution' and 'Creationism' but between 'evolution' and 'Creation-plus-microevolution'. Creation Scientists always accept some modifications in organisms over time. Yet, depending upon the explanatory potential of its causal mechanisms, it may turn out that something like *micro (with mutation, say) + time* accounts for *macro*. The boundaries of evolution cannot possibly be resolved merely by stipulation!

Hypothesis (CS-3), which holds that the Earth has experienced a worldwide flood, of course, appears to have obvious religious significance derived from the Biblical accounts of a worldwide flood. Prominent Creation Scientist Henry Morris has emphasized that belief in a worldwide flood is essential to maintaining a literal interpretation of the Bible as the inspired word of God (Morris 1974, pp. 250–52). Others have been more circumspect. In the 'Special Edition' of his work, *In the Beginning*, which is intended to present the scientific evidence for Creation and to exclude religious sources (Brown 1995), Walter Brown defends the occurrence of a worldwide flood to explain the fossil record and geological strata. Apart from its merits with respect to these phenomena, it also appears to raise more questions than it answers regarding organic evolution specifically.

Consider the problem of repopulating the earth. If every form of life (save those that thrive in oceans) was extinguished during the flood except for those who were saved by Noah and his family aboard the Ark, then if something on the order of one million land-borne species exist today—which is a very low estimate, as E.O. Wilson observes (Wilson 1992)—then these species must be descendants of species aboard the Ark, if the flood chronology is true. According to the calculations of an

Anglican Bishop, James Ussher (1581–1665), who assigned dates to Biblical events, the worldwide flood took place in 2349 B.C. There are signs of a huge flood in the Tigris-Euphrates valley that took place about 2800 B.C., but it was a local rather than a global flood (Asimov 1987).

According to Genesis, Noah built an Ark in compliance with God's specifications, the length of which was 300 cubits, the breadth 50 cubits, and the height 30 cubits, where a 'cubit' measured the length of the arm from the end of the middle finger to the elbow (or 18–22 inches). Again, following God's instructions, Noah populated the Ark with his family and a pair of each kind of living thing. God then caused it to rain upon the earth for forty days and forty nights, creating a worldwide flood of more than ten months in duration, which brought about the extinction of every single species not represented aboard the Ark—except, presumably, those that inhabited the seas. All life on Earth was then repopulated from species that survived on the Ark.

During a public lecture on the subject that I attended, Walter Brown said that Noah had taken twenty thousand animals aboard the Ark, which was created with suitable accommodations, including, for example, an exercise room for the animals. In a fascinating slip that occurs in the 'Special Edition' of his work, he maintains that dinosaur eggs "would be quite easy to handle" aboard the Ark (Brown 1995, p. 166). Whether dinosaurs would have been as easy to handle is not discussed. When the figure of 20,000 is divided by two to reflect the number of pairs of sexually reproducing species, then the maximum number of species that were aboard the Ark must have been ten thousand. If the flood occurred in 2349 B.C., while the number of species that exist today is conservatively estimated at one million, then more than 990,000 species have evolved in the interim (that is, in 4,355 years).

The temporal interval from 2349 B.C. to A.D. 2006 is 4,355 years. So an average of 225 species had to have evolved during each year, a figure that appears to be considerably more rapid than that of the cichlid fish of Lake Victoria, where three hundred species evolved in twelve thousand years, a rate of approximately one new species every forty years. Even apart from numerous other difficulties that flood chronology generates—such as the blatantly incestuous character of the repopulation of the human species by Noah's family, the problems of feeding and caring for ten thousand species (including viruses and bacteria along with animals and plants, many of which have very brief life spans and consume one another in the wild)—even elementary calculations establish that flood chronology implies the existence of an abundance of *macroevolution*.

It does not take a rocket scientist to realize that the three theses that define Creation Science in its contemporary guise—(CS-1), (CS-2), and (CH-3)—do not qualify as scientific hypotheses. Alternatively, if (CS-3), for example, is taken to be a scientific hypothesis because it can be subjected to empirical test on the basis of calculations such as those that have just been performed, then it may, at best, be said that, to the extent to which Creation Science qualifies as *science*, it does not support creation; and to the extent to which Creation Science supports *creation*, it does not qualify as science. Even without addressing a host of other problems that Creation Science raises, the distinction between *microevolution* and *macroevolution* upon which its tenability depends cannot be sustained, especially in light of the proliferation of speciation implied by flood chronology itself.

Thus, neither contemporary evaluations of Creationist hypotheses based upon the principles of inference to the best explanation nor classic evaluations based upon principles of conditionality, testability, and tentativeness (which reflects the attitude of believers toward the objects of their beliefs) support the classification of Creationist hypotheses as scientific. This does not imply that a scientist, for example, could not believe in God, but it would require that she differentiate between beliefs that she holds on scientific grounds (such as that new life forms are brought about by means of evolution) and those she holds on religious grounds (such as that God created the world and everything therein). For, if the question is raised, 'Creation or Evolution?', the answer—at this point, the only available *scientific* answer, at least—seems to be 'Creation by Evolution'.

# CHAPTER 2

# Where Is Evolution Going?

→ *Creationists routinely misrepresent evolutionary theory*

→ *Evolution does not tend toward what is best, but only toward what is good enough*

→ *'Survival of the fittest' can avoid tautology, if fitness is defined in terms of probabilities*

→ *Attempts to describe the evolutionary process as one of solving algorithms are misconceived*

→ *Sometimes evolution is progressive and sometimes it isn't*

$T$he species of Creationism that we have considered, including classic Creationism and Creation Science, are not exhaustive of the genus. Henry Morris, for example, offers an alternative version in his Scientific Creationism (1974, p. 12). Morris distinguishes the 'evolution model' from the 'Creation model':

**Table 2.1** Morris's Evolution and Creation Models

| EVOLUTION MODEL | CREATION MODEL |
| --- | --- |
| Continuing naturalistic origin | Completed supernatural origin |
| Net present increase in complexity | Net present decrease in complexity |

At least two aspects of these 'models' should be immediately apparent: first, that the distinction between 'naturalistic' and 'super-naturalistic' origins, causes, or creators implies that the evolution model may be scientific, but the Creation model cannot be; and, second, that there appears to be heavy reliance upon considerations related to the second law of thermodynamics, except that now increases in entropy are identified with decreases in complexity and *vice versa*.

We discovered already in the Prologue that global increases in entropy were consistent with local decreases in entropy. It should come as no surprise that the same must hold true for complexity, when complexity is identified with entropy. Thus, local increases in complexity are compatible with global decreases in complexity. A closely related idea is that any cause must be greater than its effects. When we think of the natural world as a totality, this principle seems to imply that it must have a greater supernatural cause or Creator. Many examples—including the zygote that develops into a human being, the acorn that develops into a mighty oak, and such—suggest that this principle does not hold for open systems. But even were this principle to hold for closed systems, what follows is not that Creationism is science but that science cannot study Creation.

The evolution of complexity arises again and again in Creationist literature, ranging in forms from gross falsehood to subtle distortion. Walter Brown (1995, p. 15) maintains that evolution "is a theory without a mechanism [to bring about more complex from less complex forms of life]." Those who have read Chapter 2 will probably be able to recognize how gross a falsehood this really is. Elsewhere (Brown 1995, p. 172), however, he offers the following diagram, which purports to be a comparison

**Figure 2.1** Brown's Comparison of Creation and Evolution

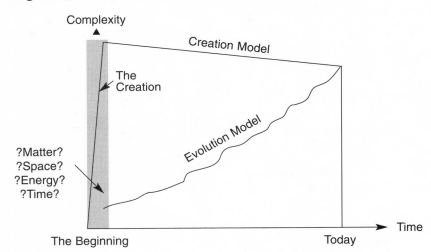

of Creation and evolution on the complexity scale. What may be most striking about this 'comparison', however, is its scale. The top-line represents a time-line of about ten thousand years for Creationism, while the bottom-line represents a time-line of about five billion years for the age of Earth. If the bottom-line were drawn to the same 'scale' as is the top line, then the bottom-line would turn out to be more than fifteen miles long!

The difference, of course, is that the slope that represents increasing complexity for evolution would be very slight, not at all as it is represented here. More interesting than this sleight-of-hand, however, is that Creation models quite generally assume that the moment of Creation was the moment of greatest complexity or of greatest perfection; consequently, whatever comes thereafter must reflect a loss of complexity or a diminution of perfection through a process of deterioration. It implies that primitive humans were more advanced than modern humans, that earlier forms of life were more developed than later forms of life, and so on. This may sound highly counterintuitive, but science cannot be constrained by intuition. If evolution promotes progress, then we would expect the opposite to be the case, where modern humans would be more advanced than primitive humans and later forms of life more developed than earlier forms of life. If evolution always brings about optimal solutions to problems of adaptation, then evolution must be progressive. But whether that is the case remains to be seen. Perhaps evolutionary progress is a myth.

## 2.1 *The Tautology Problem*

One controversial issue among evolutionary theorists is whether evolution is in any sense an optimizing process—a process tending towards improvement or progress. In *The Latest on the Best*, a collection of articles on this disputed question, some who believe that evolution should be viewed as an optimizing process join issues with others who do not. As the editor John Dupre observes,

> A number of the contributors from the earlier parts of the anthology . . . argue forcefully for the difficulties with any general assumption that evolution generates optimal adaptation. On the other hand, a number of the contributors involved in applications of optimality analysis are extremely enthusiastic about the potential benefits of this approach. (Dupre 1987, p. 22)

As Dupre also points out, even within biology itself there appears to be more enthusiasm for applications of optimality theory than there is for the conclusion that evolution itself is an optimizing process (Dupre 1987, p. 22).

Let's think about this issue by exploring the differences between optimizing and satisficing approaches toward understanding evolution. 'Satisficing' means tending only to what is 'good enough', rather than what is ideally best. In the process, we shall have to deal with the claim that satisficing has no clear meaning in evolutionary theory. By focusing upon the probabilistic character of fitness, however, it ought to be possible to shed light upon these difficult problems, since neither of the two most adequate accounts of probability as a physical property—the frequency interpretation and the propensity interpretation—support the conception of evolution as an optimizing process.

My general conception is that evolutionary selection takes place relative to adaptations that are 'good enough' to sustain survival and reproduction. While optimizing theory can play a valuable heuristic function in suggesting hypotheses about the design of organisms, satisficing theory affords a more adequate framework for understanding the broadest and deepest features of evolution as a process.

The issues encountered within this domain are closely related, if not identical, to those that revolve about the suitability of the phrase, 'survival of the fittest', as a general depiction of the evolutionary process. As Ernst Mayr observes, Charles Darwin borrowed the phrase from Herbert Spencer (Mayr 1982, Sections 386 and 519). If those who survive are the fittest, then the process of natural selection should invariably produce increasingly fit organisms across time, and there can be no basis for doubting whether the latest must be the best. If biological evolution is a process that invariably induces the survival of the best, then it must be impossible for the latest not to be the best.

Although Mayr is concerned that the phrase 'survival of the fittest' may be merely tautological as a claim that cannot be false by virtue of its meaning, when properly understood, it not only appears to be no tautology but may even be empirically false. The problem is to separate the meaning of 'fitness' from the meaning of 'those who survive', which may be accomplished by viewing 'fitness' as a probabilistic tendency to survive and reproduce. (A closely related view is proposed in Sober 1984, Chapter 2.) When the exact character of this probabilistic tendency is rendered more precise, however, it then becomes evident that 'high fitness' may or may not be associated with increased frequency for survival and reproduction.

Although we shall pursue more exact characterizations in the following, it may be worthwhile to provide a general sketch of the differences that tend to distinguish 'optimizing' from 'satisficing'. These notions are derived from decision theory, where optimizing models characterize systems that always select solutions to problems that are at least as 'good' as any other solution; satisficing models, by comparison, characterize systems that select solutions to problems that are 'good enough' but which may have alternatives that are even better. Judgments of goodness (good, better, and best), of course, are relative to some presupposed set of values or utilities. (Michalos 1973 provides an illuminating introduction to these alternatives.)

When these ideas are applied within the context of evolutionary theory, however, an important distinction must be drawn. Decision theory is normative and prescribes how people should act, whereas evolutionary theory is explanatory and describes how nature works. While normative theories do not have to be abandoned or be repaired when they do not describe the way things are, explanatory theories in science must be abandoned or be repaired when they do not describe the way things are. If nature does not operate in conformity with optimizing models, then that counts against their standing as scientific theories, although optimizing models for decision-making are not thereby disqualified, even if no one acts in conformity with them.

The values or utilities that are commonly assumed to possess evolutionary significance, no doubt, are those of survival and reproduction, especially offspring production equal to or greater than replacement level. Relative to this measure of utility, organism $x$ may be supposed to have 'higher fitness' than organism $y$, with respect to a specific environment, for example, when $x$ has greater probability of offspring production than $y$, with respect to that environment. As Elliott Sober has observed, there are good reasons to resist the temptation of identifying 'fitness' in this sense with actual reproductive success, since this property seems to be best envisioned as a disposition toward reproduction in lieu of its actual obtainment (Sober 1984, pp. 43–44).

Since nature cannot be expected to select solutions to problems that are unavailable, whether or not evolution should be viewed as an optimizing or as a satisficing process must be relative to the available gene pool and the available environment rather than relative to every possible gene pool and every possible environment. If these stronger conceptions are taken to describe kinds of 'global optimality', then only weaker conceptions of 'local optimality' deserve consideration here. Evolution would appear to qualify as an optimizing process in the appropriate sense, therefore, so long as selection produces organisms with fitness values that are equal to or greater than those of parent generations across time, relative to these constraints.

To ascertain whether or not evolution ought to be viewed as an optimizing or as a satisficing process, therefore, it is essential to secure the right kind of non-tautological connection between 'fitness' and 'those who survive' and then to determine if the resulting process is optimizing, satisficing, or something else instead. If the less fit sometimes survive and reproduce while the more fit do not, for example, then surely that is something that evolutionary theory ought to be able to explain. Ultimately, it seems, evolution needs to be understood by means of the repetitive operation of 'single case' tendencies for particular traits to be selected under specific (possibly unique) conditions utilizing the idea of single-case propensities.

This conception, however, should not be confused with the notion of single-step selection in the sense that Richard Dawkins has introduced, where entities or organisms are sorted once and for all (Dawkins 1986, pp. 45–46). Single-case propensities as properties of specific events are compatible with cumulative selection operating across time, while single-step selection is not. As Dawkins himself has observed,

> There is a big difference . . . between cumulative selection (in which each improvement, however slight, is used as a basis for future building), and single-step selection (in which each new 'try' is a fresh one). If evolution had to rely on single-step selection, it would never have got anywhere. (Dawkins 1986, p. 49)

The application of the propensity interpretation to the problem at hand, therefore, should not be rejected on the ground that evolution is a cumulative rather than a single-step process.

In their valuable paper on optimality theory in evolutionary biology, G.A. Parker and J. Maynard Smith, both noted for their contributions to this domain, consider the question, 'Can natural selection optimize?' In their view, optimization by natural selection requires special conditions, because the potential for optimization by means of natural selection depends on gene expression (the phenotypic manifestations of underlying genes) and on mechanisms for genetic change in populations, such as the rate at which natural selection has the capacity to alter genetic structure, the amount of additive genetic variance present at the start of selection, gene flow (for example, that arising from immigration), the rate at which conditions change, and random effects such as genetic drift. Moreover,

> Most optimality models assume that strategies reproduce asexually, or if the model is Mendelian, that the optimal prototype can breed true. Pleiotropy [genes affecting multiple traits] is assumed not to operate and strategies are allowed to replicate independently of each other. Obviously selection cannot produce an optimum if there is no way of achieving it genetically, but for some models, it is clear that selection will get as close to the optimum as the genetic mechanism will allow. (Parker and Maynard Smith 1990, pp. 30–31)

When natural selection occurs in asexually reproducing or true breeding populations within stable environments that endure unchanged for periods of time sufficient for optimal traits to emerge, optimizing models of evolution may be appropriate, in the absence of pleiotropic effects. In situations of the kind that characterize most natural as opposed to artificial environments, however, conditions like these are not realized.

Indeed, even Parker and Maynard Smith themselves observe that the emergence of optimal traits is not easily arranged: "infinite time and infinite populations would be needed to achieve the [evolutionary] peak itself" (Parker and Maynard Smith 1990, p. 31). But this means that optimality theory provides an idealized conception of what might happen in the limit as a special case rather than a descriptive explanatory framework for understanding evolution under normal conditions. A satisficing model, by comparison, provides a foundation for viewing the emergence of optimal adaptations as a possible long-run product of what has to be understood as a short-run process that applies to finite populations and finite times.

The tendency in evolutionary theory to focus on the long run rather than on the short run or on the single case has a parallel in the theory of probability itself, where long-run frequency conceptions have prevailed until recently. The emergence of the single-case propensity conception within this context thus promises to shed light on natural selection. Indeed, from the perspective afforded by the single-case propensity conception, appeals to the ultimate outcome of long-run processes appear to have the general character of teleological causation, whereas appeals to the proximate outcomes of single-case processes appear to have the general character of mechanistic causation instead (Fetzer 1988a).

If optimal adaptations only emerge as a special limiting case under quite idealized conditions, moreover, it should be evident that the products of evolution that emerge during any merely finite segment of the world's history are never optimal, unless allowance is made for their production as a consequence of fortuitous conditions (or by chance). But if this is indeed the case, then satisficing appears to be the strongest theory that generally applies. While Parker and Maynard Smith consider "the comparative method" and "quantitative genetics," they do not consider satisficing approaches at all. Once the properties of satisficing models are properly understood, however, their appeal should become obvious.

Evolution appears to be an inherently probabilistic process, at least to the extent to which sexual selection, sexual reproduction, genetic drift and the like involve probabilistic elements. Two interpretations of probability might apply here, the long-run frequency interpretation, which identifies probabilities with limiting frequencies in infinite sequences, and the single case propensity conception, which identifies them with the strengths of causal tendencies to bring about particular outcomes on individual trials. While we have already discovered that optimal adaptations as a result of natural selection only occur (other than by chance) over the long run, perhaps evolution can still be viewed as a probabilistically optimizing process.

Suppose we define 'fitness' in terms of probability of survival and reproduction at a level equal to or greater than replacement level R within the specific environment E. Thus, if the probability for survival and reproduction R within environment E is greater for individual $x$ than it is for individual $y$, then there are properties of $x$ (which here are not specified) in relation to the properties of $y$ (also unspecified) such that $x$ is more fit than $y$ with respect to R within E. Then it might be plausible to hold that less fit traits will decrease in frequency across time or that less fit traits will eventually no longer be 'good enough' to sustain survival and reproduction. But when such claims are subjected to close scrutiny in relation to the frequency and the propensity alternatives, it becomes clear that they cannot be sustained. Even when claims about what will probably occur displace claims about what will occur, these probabilistic alternatives do not support the idea of evolution as an optimizing process.

On the frequency interpretation of probability, for example, the probability for B in relation to A equals $n$—that is, $P(B/A) = n$—if and only if the limiting frequency for B in an infinite sequence of A trials equals $n$. The relative frequency for B in finite segments of A trials can arbitrarily vary from $n$. Whenever $P(B/A) = n$, of course, $P(-B/A) = 1 - n$. Even if $n$ is high and $1 - n$ is low, outcomes with low probability can occur, even with high relative frequency, across any finite segment of the world's history. While the frequency interpretation guarantees convergence between probabilities and frequencies over the long run, it does not guarantee convergence of probabilities and frequencies in the short run.

If we identify outcomes of kind B with offspring production at equal to or greater than replacement level relative to environments of kind A, then it should be apparent that, even when that outcome has high probability, the result of offspring production at less than replacement level may still occur, over the short run, in relation to the frequency approach. Moreover, if we identify outcomes of kind B instead with the production of offspring whose own fitness values are equal to or greater than those of their parents, then it should still be apparent that, even when that outcome has high probability, the result of the production of offspring whose own fitness values are less than those of their parents may likewise occur.

On the propensity interpretation of probability, matters are even worse, since, as a property of each single trial of those conditions, even infinitely many repetitions of those conditions cannot guarantee that an outcome will occur with a limiting frequency that equals its generating propensity. This interpretation maintains that the probability for B in relation to A equals $n$ if and only if there is a causal tendency of strength $n$ for conditions A to produce (or 'bring about') an outcome of kind B on any single trial of that kind which might be represented formally employing the (probabilistic) causal conditional, '. . . $=n=>$ ___', where '$(x)(t)(Axt =n=> Bxt^*)$' means the strength of the tendency for a single trial of kind A at $t$ to bring about outcome B at $t^*$ is $n$. The conditions that specify a trial of kind A can be broadly construed to include conceptions and gestations that endure over intervals of time so long as every property that is relevant to the outcome is considered (Boyd 1997).

The ontological difference between the frequency and the propensity interpretations is that one makes probabilities properties of infinite sequences while the other makes them properties of singular trials. The advantage of the propensity approach, from this point of view, is that, if the world's history is merely finite, the existence of probabilities as propensities remains secure, while the existence of probabilities as frequencies is problematical. The logical connection that obtains between probabilities and frequencies on the frequency approach, however, is completely severed by the propensity approach, since, even over infinite sequences of trials, the limiting frequency for outcome B might deviate arbitrarily from the propensity for B.

## 2.2 *Does Evolution Optimize?*

Three possible foundations for the conception of evolution as an optimizing process have been considered, none of which provides suitable support. The first came from Parker and Maynard Smith's discussion of the conditions that are required for natural selection to produce optimal adaptations. When natural selection occurs in asexually reproducing or true breeding populations within stable environments that endure unchanged for periods of time that are sufficient for optimal traits to emerge, optimizing models of evolution can be applied in the absence of pleiotropic effects. Most natural situations do not satisfy the conditions, however, and optimal adaptations require infinite populations and time.

This means that optimality theory provides an idealized conception of what might happen in the limit as a special case rather than a descriptive explanatory framework for understanding evolution under normal conditions. Moreover, appealing to probabilistic properties does not appear to salvage the situation. Under the frequency interpretation, higher fitness yields higher frequencies of survival and reproduction (or higher fitness in offspring generations) only by assuming infinite sequences of trials. Under the propensity interpretation, higher fitness affords no guarantee of higher frequencies of survival and reproduction (or higher fitness in offspring generations) even if infinite sequences are assumed.

Probabilistic factors are a source of difficulties for the conception of evolution as an optimizing process, especially in relation to the mechanism of natural selection, but they are not the only source of difficulties. Others include different ways in which various environments can be subject to change, which I'll refer to here as 'random happenings' and as 'accidental occurrences':

(i)  Random happenings (such as stray bullets, terrorist bombs, and
     the AIDS virus) are micro properties which vary within macro
     environments. None of us has greater fitness in coping with them
     as a rule, but only some of us actually encounter them. Organisms
     with high fitness within macro environments may not survive
     and reproduce due to their influence, while organisms with low
     fitness within those macro environments may do so.

(ii) Accidental occurrences (including large asteroids hitting the
     Earth) are events that bring about major alterations in the macro
     environment, which we otherwise tend to treat as a 'closed sys-
     tem'. Once again, organisms with high fitness within macro envi-
     ronments may not survive to reproduce due to their influence, as
     may have happened with the dinosaurs. Other organisms of lower
     fitness, however, might nonetheless survive.

The point of introducing these concepts is not to suggest that evolutionary theoreticians have been oblivious to the role of random factors or of
accidental occurrences as they have been defined above (which Arnold
and Fristrup 1982, among others, have acknowledged), but rather that
they indicate historical difficulties in securing the conditions that must
obtain for optimizing models to apply. If the conditions under which natural selection operates are constantly changing due to the influence of
random factors and of accidental occurrences, then reliance upon models
that presuppose infinite populations across infinite times relative to
unchanging environments cannot provide an adequate foundation for
describing or explaining the actual course of the evolutionary process.

Perhaps the most important difference between optimizing and satisficing theory, from this perspective, is that optimizing theory implies that,
over the long run, if not the short, organisms become increasingly more
and more fit as a result of an inevitable 'winnowing process' that takes
place within constant environments. Satisficing theory, however, carries
no such implication, accepting instead that sometimes higher fitness may
not increase in relative frequency across time, while lower fitness does.
The satisficing approach, nevertheless, provides a foundation for viewing
the emergence of optimal adaptations as a possible 'long-run' product of
what has to be understood as a 'short run' process that applies to finite
populations and finite times, under certain highly fortuitious conditions.

Other authors, especially Susan Mills and John Beatty, have proposed
that the propensity interpretation of probability might provide an appropriate foundation for understanding the nature of fitness (Mills and

Beatty 1979). Their conception, however, does not properly represent either the context-dependence of propensities or their character as single-case causal tendencies. Consequently, they encounter difficulty in developing an adequate account of fitness as a propensity, which leads them to reconsider the adequacy of this approach (Beatty and Feinsen 1989). The difficulties they consider, however, appear to be problems with the notion of fitness rather than problems with the notion of propensities, when that conception is properly understood (see Fetzer 1986).

Some of the most important reservations that have been raised concerning propensities, moreover, concern their formal properties. Beatty and Feinsen (1989), for example, assume that propensities are properly formalized as conditional probabilities and that there must be a positive correlation between high fitness and reproductive success. These assumptions, which others, such as Alexander Rosenberg and Robert Brandon, have endorsed, provide a misleading characterization of the propensity interpretation and generate problems that are more apparent than real (see Fetzer 1981; Niiniluoto 1988). Other objections are also defeated by the failure to appreciate that any probability measures constructed on the basis of the propensity interpretation qualify as propensity concepts.

While the foregoing arguments may already provide forceful evidence that evolution is not an optimizing process, I want to advance at least one additional argument to make it very obvious that there are evolutionary phenomena that cannot be appropriately understood on the basis of an optimizing model but which make good sense from the point of view of satisficing. This case has been offered by David S. Wilson (1980), who suggests that there is nothing about evolutionary theory that precludes the possibility that selection might 'routinely' occur under conditions whereby an organism $x$ decreases its own fitness but nevertheless is selected because it has decreased the fitness of competing conspecifics $y$ even more (Wilson 1980 as reprinted in Brandon and Burian 1984, p. 275).

An appropriate analogy is American political campaigns, where negative advertising is normally judged successful as long as it enhances relative differences. There is an instructive lesson for evolutionary theory here, moreover, since cases of this kind emphasize that selection tends to be a matter of relative rather than of absolute fitness, insofar as those traits that confer a competitive advantage with respect to survival and reproduction can be 'good enough' even if better solutions are available. If organisms can benefit from diminishing their fitness in order to increase their relative advantage over others, then it is difficult to see how the idea of evolution as an optimizing process can be justified.

It could be maintained that, even if natural selection (or evolution, which is not confined to the mechanisms of natural selection) is not an optimizing process, optimality theory remains a useful heuristic device for generating hypotheses about phenotypic design, even if "not about the process of evolution that produced that design" (Smith 1991b). In suggesting this alternative, Eric Smith admits that there may be significant philosophical questions that can be raised about using optimality theory to study something, such as phenotypic design, that is the result of a non-optimizing process, but he cites the publication of thousands of research articles in which optimality theory fulfills precisely such a role.

In advancing this position, Smith would seem to echo the findings of John Dupre, when he reports that within biology itself there appears to be more enthusiasm for applications of optimality theory than exists for the conclusion that evolution itself is an optimizing process (Dupre 1987, p. 22). And, indeed, the potential for optimality theory to fulfill a role in generating hypotheses about degrees of adaptiveness of phenotypes relative to specific environments does not contradict or undermine the view that fitness should be properly understood as a single-case dispositional property, where a clear distinction is drawn between fitness values and reproductive success. Optimality theory can be useful in a heuristic role.

The question of whether evolution is an optimizing process, therefore, has to be distinguished from the question of whether optimality analysis can be useful in generating fitness hypotheses. Treating nature 'as if' it were an optimizing process may be beneficial as a heuristic technique, but that does not mean that evolution itself is an optimizing process. The issue here is closely related to the distinction between realism and instrumentalism as it arises in theorizing generally. Instrumentalism views theories as instruments of prediction that are not meant to describe entities or properties in the world, while realism views theories as descriptions of the world. Optimality theory can be useful instrumentally.

Thousands of published handbooks of navigation begin with a sentence which says, 'For present purposes, we will assume that the Earth is a small stationary sphere whose center coincides with that of a much larger rotating stellar sphere', as Thomas Kuhn has observed (Kuhn 1957). The widespread utility of adopting a certain model for a special purpose, however, in no way alters the limitations of that model for understanding the world itself. If evolution is not an optimizing process, then it makes no difference that, for certain special purposes, we can treat it 'as if' it were. As long as our purpose is to understand the nature of evolution, therefore, optimizing theory is not enough. Its value appears to be exclusively heuristic.

To avoid any misunderstanding of the nature of my argument, bear in mind that evolution has several distinct dimensions. It can be viewed as a causal process involving interaction between organisms with different degrees of fitness and their environments. Since more fit organisms, by hypothesis, have higher probabilities of survival and reproduction, given a probabilistic conception of fitness, it would be mistaken to suppose that I am denying something that cannot be false. More fit organisms clearly do have higher probabilities of survival and reproduction, even if, as we have found, there is no guarantee that the traits of organisms with higher fitness will invariably increase in their relative frequencies across time.

What I am asserting instead is that the actual course of evolution that emerges depends upon an interaction between organisms and their environment, where the environment is almost constantly changing. There are at least three reasons why environmental variations tend to defeat the emergence of optimal adaptations. Because actual environments only remain constant over finite intervals, not for infinite durations; because random happenings and accidental occurrences are exerting their influence on the course of evolution; and because those who survive and reproduce may be merely the lucky rather than the fit, the process of evolution across time appears to be but a gamble with life where players shift from game to game without any advance warning.

The strongest arguments supporting the conception of evolution as an optimizing process thus appear to be indefensible. The classic model advanced by Parker and Maynard Smith depends on special conditions that are seldom, if ever, satisfied during the history of world, including, for example, infinite populations and infinite times. Two probabilistic models are available on the basis of the frequency and the propensity interpretations. The frequency-based model, however, can only guarantee that higher fitness will produce higher reproductive success over the infinite long run. And the propensity-based model cannot guarantee the convergence of fitness and success even over infinite long runs.

Evolution should not be viewed as an optimizing process. Sometimes higher fitness occurs with higher frequency across time, but sometimes not. The role of random factors and accidental happenings reinforces the variability of environments, which by itself undermines the applicability of optimality models. Nevertheless, optimality theory does appear to be applicable in the heuristic role of suggesting hypotheses about the adaptiveness of phenotypic 'designs' in generating fitness hypotheses. Taken altogether, therefore, the question of whether evolution should be viewed as an optimizing process seems to have a definite answer. Evolution is really nature gambling with life.

As Robert Richardson (1998), has observed, satisficing substitutes a 'stopping rule' for one maximizing the outcome of interest, where searching stops when a solution at a certain threshold is attained. If optimizing models characterize systems or processes that always select solutions to problems that are at least as 'good' as any other solution, while satisficing models characterize systems or processes that select solutions to problems that are 'good enough' but can still have alternatives that are even better, then evolution is clearly not an optimizing process. Nature thus appears to operate by finding solutions that are good enough rather than the best.

Survival requires finding solutions to problems. If those who survive are not necessarily the fittest, the process of natural selection may or may not produce increasingly fit organisms across time. Since biological evolution is not a process that invariably induces the survival of the best, it remains entirely possible that the latest are not the best. And insofar as natural selection and biological evolution do occur even in the absence of optimal strategies and optimal adaptations, it appears as though nature is content with genetic combinations and selection processes that are simply 'good enough'. Selection and evolution operate relative to available genes and available environments that satisfy their own non-optimal conditions.

## 2.3 *Is Evolution Algorithmic?*

The history of science reflects crucial shifts from the teleological worldview associated with Aristotle to the mechanistic worldview associated with Newton, on the one hand, and from the deterministic worldview associated with classical mechanics to the indeterministic worldview associated with quantum mechanics, on the other. Both deterministic and indeterministic worldviews, however, are mechanistic in their general character, whereas determinism presumes that laws of nature invariably bring about the same outcomes under the same conditions, while indeterminism affirms that some laws probabilistically produce one or another outcome in the same class of outcomes under the same conditions. Those familiar with the history of science may find it somewhat surprising to discover that, within several domains of current inquiry, assumptions are being adopted that not only contravene indeterministic principles but are stronger than deterministic ones in the novel guise of the contention that evolution is 'an algorithmic process'.

The first of these is the philosophy of biology. In *Darwin's Dangerous Idea* (1995), Daniel Dennett maintains that the theory of evolution by natural selection qualifies as "a dangerous idea," precisely because it provides a framework for understanding evolution as an algorithmic procedure. The second is within cognitive science, where the dominating paradigm, known as the computational conception, takes for granted that minds either are computers or, at some suitable level, operate by means of the same algorithmic principles that govern computing machines—even as a matter of definition (von Eckhardt 1993). And a third arises within what is called evolutionary psychology, where Leda Cosmides and John Tooby, especially, maintain that human reasoning is under the control of Darwinian algorithms as mental procedures that have evolved by natural selection (Cosmides 1985; 1989; Cosmides and Tooby 1987).

Their apparent convergence upon the centrality of algorithms within these domains, however, does not guarantee that cognitive science, the philosophy of biology, and evolutionary psychology therefore rest upon a firm foundation. For reasons that I have elsewhere explained, neither cognitive science nor evolutionary psychology seems to be theoretically well-grounded. The computational conception, for example, appears to represent a striking over-generalization of one rather special kind of thinking that does not seem to be characteristic of human thought processes generally (Fetzer 1994; 1997; 1998a). As a theory of reasoning specifically rather than of thinking, evolutionary psychology inherits only some of these problems, but it also confronts difficulties of its own (Davies, Fetzer, and Foster 1995; Fetzer 2005). My purpose here is to explore the extent to which evolutionary biology itself fits within an algorithmic framework.

The classic conception of algorithms characterizes them as effective decision procedures, which are methods or techniques that can be applied to problems of appropriate kinds to yield correct solutions within a finite sequence of steps (Kleene 1967, Chapter 5). Because algorithms have these properties, they are definite (you always get an answer), reliable (you always get a correct answer) and completable (you always get a correct answer in a finite interval of time). According to the computational conception, therefore, thought processses are governed by mental algorithms. Dreams and daydreams, however, appear to be instances of ordinary thought processes that have neither definite beginnings nor definite endings and that do not provide reliable solutions to problems, if they provide 'solutions' to 'problems' at all. They are among several kinds of non-algorithmic thought processes that undermine the computational conception.

The wide variety of phenomena that tend to disconfirm or even refute the dominating paradigm include (a) that thinking does not require the execution of mental algorithms, because imagination and conjecture (including dreams and daydreams) involve thought but do not require the execution of mental algorithms, (b) that some kinds of reasoning (involving the use of heuristic procedures or asymmetrical decision methods) are kinds of reasoning that do not require the execution of any algorithm, (c) that ordinary thinking displays probabilistic associations of thoughts that do not qualify as algorithmic or even as partially-algorithmic, and (d) that even the availability of marks as subject to systematic syntactical manipulation apparently presupposes the existence of interpretations, interpreters or minds, which takes for granted what computational conceptions are intended to explain. It cannot be sustained (Fetzer 2000).

The problems with evolutionary psychology do not arise from the general appeal to evolutionary influences as causal determinants of mental abilities but rather from the specific form that these mental abilities are supposed to assume as Darwinian algorithms. If mental processes are properly viewed as causal but non-algorithmic, where some kinds of reasoning, but not thinking generally, may have an algorithmic character, then those who take for granted that thought processes are algorithmic— even apart from their adaptive character—have committed a blunder. Thus, the research program advocated by Cosmides and Tooby can be improved by embracing the conception of epigenetic rules as genetically programmed, species-specific developmental tendencies that may or may not be algorithmic (Alexander 1990; Davies, Fetzer, and Foster 1995; Fetzer 1991/96).

Dennett invites us to view evolution by natural selection as an algorithmic process, where (in his words) "an algorithm is a certain sort of formal process that can be counted on—logically—to yield a certain sort of result whenever it is 'run' or instantiated" (Dennett 1995, p. 50). The key features of algorithms are said to be substrate neutrality (they can be implemented by many different kinds of systems), underlying mindlessness (they can be applied mechanically without thought or judgment), and guaranteed results (they always provide reliable solutions to the problems to which they apply). Their characterization as 'formal processes' thus reflects their substrate neutrality. Darwin's dangerous idea is then paraphrased by Dennett in the following fashion: "Life on Earth has been generated over billions of years in a single branching tree—the Tree of Life—by one algorithmic process or another" (Dennett 1995, p. 51).

The 'Tree of Life', as a branching tree structure that reflects the history of species across time, must be understood as the product of causal mechanisms of various kinds applied to the specific conditions that obtained during specific intervals through the history of life on Earth. These causal mechanisms include genetic mutation, sexual reproduction, genetic drift, and genetic engineering (as sources of genetic variation) and natural selection, sexual selection, group selection and artificial selection (as related mechanisms of selection). Thus, 'natural selection' has both a broad and a narrow sense, where in its broad sense, 'natural selection' includes all these less artificial selection and genetic engineering, perhaps, but in its narrow sense, 'natural selection' applies to competition between con-specifics as individuals.

Strictly speaking, for evolution by natural selection (in its broad sense) to be algorithmic, it would have to be the case that each of the causal mechanisms for variation and for selection that have been mentioned qualify as 'algorithmic' in the appropriate sense. Specifically, it would have to be the case that, for each instance of operation of each of these causal mechanisms during the course of life on Earth, they satisfy the requirements for being effective decision procedures—or Dennett's counterpart conditions of substrate neutrality, underlying mindlessness and guaranteed results. If genetic mutation, sexual reproduction and sexual selection, for example, do not qualify as effective decision procedures that bring about guaranteed results, then natural selection (in its broad sense) cannot properly qualify as 'algorithmic' and Dennett will have misdescribed it.

That algorithmic processes have a definite beginning ('input') and a definite ending ('output') follows from their character as effective decision procedures. While Dennett asserts that "Every computer program is an algorithm" (Dennett 1995, p. 51), he also acknowledges that, in his sense, 'an algorithm' need not terminate (Dennett 1995, p. 52, note 8). It would be better, however, to preserve the distinction between 'programs' and 'algorithms' where 'programs' incorporate algorithms in causal forms suitable for execution by organisms or by machines. In this case, algorithms could retain their character as effective decision procedures (abstractly specified), while programs would be causal incorporations that might suffer from failures due inadequate implementations. Algorithms then specify procedures, while mechanisms incorporate processes.

The inconsistency in maintaining that natural selection is an 'algorithmic' process guaranteed to yield successful results, on the one hand, and that some 'algorithms' are properly so-called even though they never terminate, on the other, displays itself in the realization that non-termination does not ordinarily yield what would be viewed as a successful outcome. Perhaps some 'problems' are better left 'unsolved', but for the remainder, non-termination does not qualify as 'a solution to a problem'!

It should be obvious, moreover, that at least some of the causal mechanisms that are subsumed by natural selection (in its broad sense)—including genetic mutation and sexual reproduction, for example—are typically
regarded as probabilistic (or 'indeterministic') causal processes where their
operation can produce one or another outcome—such as mutation/non-
mutation or genotype1/genotype2—under the same conditions.

This is a striking result on several counts. In the first place, it is not
clear why one or another of these outcomes would be viewed as 'successful' and the other as 'unsuccessful'. Without such a standard, however, it is
impossible to tell whether or not a process yields a 'successful' result. If
ninety-eight perecent of all species have become extinct, for example, is
extinction then a 'success'? In the second place, the very possibility of
more than one possible outcome ('output') under the same conditions
('input') places the very idea of 'algorithmic process' into doubt.
Algorithmic procedures, after all, have to be implemented by means of
deterministic processes, since otherwise they cannot be guaranteed to
produce 'solutions', such as, say, survival and reproduction. There appear
to be ample grounds to conclude not only that natural selection (in either
sense) is not an algorithmic procedure but that it is also not a deterministic process. Dennett's formulations, however, obscure the importance of
this fundamental connection.

Dennett contends that, while some algorithms are "guaranteed to do
whatever they do," others are "guaranteed to tend (with probability $n$) to
do something" (Dennett 1995, p. 57). He appears to be appealing implicitly to a single-case propensity conception. Yet once beyond the domain
of determinism, no process can properly qualify as 'algorithmic'.
Algorithms are technically defined as functions understood as classes of
ordered pairs, which map values in some domain of values $x$ onto those
of some range of values $y$ (Boas 1960, p. 65). Thus, an output $y$ is a function of an input $x$ if, when $x$ is given, the value of $y$ is uniquely determined. Non-deterministic processes do not satisfy this conception,
because they provide either no value or more than one value for the output $y$ for at least some values of input $x$. Processes that fail to provide
solutions for problems that are uniquely determined for each value of
input $x$ thus cannot qualify as 'algorithmic' (Fetzer 1994a, pp. 2–5, 10–13).

Dennett's attenuated sense of this term does not even correspond to
that of a partial function understood as a partial mapping from a domain
$x$ to a range $y$ which is unique for each value of $x$ when a corresponding
value of $y$ happens to exist. In this sense, partial functions are incomplete
classes of ordered pairs, but they retain the uniqueness condition that, for
any specific value of $x$, there exists at most one corresponding value of $y$.

Processes that tend (with probability *n*) to bring about their outcomes where more than one outcome is possible, therefore, are simply non-algorithmic. Moreover, while Dennett wants to maintain that the algorithmic procedures that govern evolution are causal processes that tend to produce organisms increasingly adapted to their environments, natural selection itself does not appear to be capable of guaranteed optimal solutions to problems of adaptation—even probabilistically!

To the question, 'Is evolution progressive?', therefore, the only appropriate response appears to be, 'Sometimes it is, sometimes it isn't!', which means that the answer is, 'Not necessarily!' While it is physically possible for later species be more fit than earlier species, the influence of random factors and of accidental occurrences combine with the probabilistic character of evolutionary causal mechanisms to preclude any guarantees. Sexual reproduction, sexual selection, and genetic drift, for example, contribute to create conditions under which the operation of evolution can be appropriately described as 'a gamble with life'. Although appeals to algorithms are currently surfacing in various domains, the causal mechanisms encompassed thereby are not always definite, reliable, and completable. The evolution of species—including speciation and extinction—is no more governed by algorithmic processes than it is governed by optimizing ones.

It does not follow that evolution precludes the possibility of progress, when measured on the basis of appropriate biological criteria. The causal mechanisms of evolution, especially natural selection, tend to promote fitness in organisms, but there are no built-in guarantees. Just as short-term increases in complexity are physically compatible with long-term increases in entropy, short term increases in adaptiveness are physically compatible with long-term—even abrupt—extinction, which all species are destined to suffer, sooner or later. It would therefore be a mistake to maintain that 'Darwinism denies progress', as Michael Ruse has recently proclaimed (Ruse 1998, p. 93).

It would be better to observe that Darwinism cannot guarantee progress than that it denies progress. That evolution cannot guarantee progress does not mean that it denies progress, which Ruse, perhaps the leading authority on the concept of progress in evolutionary theory in the world today, understands perfectly well. That evolution guarantees progress and that evolution denies progress are contraries, which can both be false, rather than contradictories, of which one or the other must be true.

In *Monad to Man* (1996), Ruse suggests that progressivism continues to exert a subtle but powerful influence upon professional biologists, where comparisons between popular writings and scientific publications tend to support the conclusion that the idea of progress has been promoted primarily by religious, political, and other cultural forces. And he's absolutely right to maintain—as he does here and elsewhere—that the discovery that human beings are the product of a natural process qualifies as the most important self-discovery of our history. Darwin's conception was a dangerous idea, not because it was algorithmic, but because it did not require a Creator.

CHAPTER 3

# Let's See Some ID

➻ *Aside from the age of the Earth, Creation Science is committed to a world-wide flood five thousand years ago, in which all land animals not taken by Noah onto the Ark were destroyed*

➻ *The failure of Creation Science to bring Creation into the science classroom has led to Intelligent Design (ID), a Creationist movement with more modest claims and a broader constituency*

➻ *ID rests on an imperfect and misplaced appeal to the analogy of a human designer*

➻ *The alternative to ID is not 'chance', but the interaction of an element of chance with law-governed causal processes*

➻ *Courts have found abundant evidence that the campaign to include ID in public school science teaching is religiously motivated*

Creation Science claims to qualify as a science. But in making this claim it runs into a dilemma, even if we apply the simple criteria that scientific hypotheses are conditional, testable, and tentative.

The thesis of a young Earth, for example, (CS-1), can be formulated to accommodate the present state of the world, no matter what, in which case it cannot qualify as scientific because it is not empirically testable. Alternatively, however, when formulated on the basis of some specification of the age of the Earth, such as ten thousand years, it turns out to be richly testable in many different ways, and provably false. Many different findings from astronomy, cosmology, geology, and paleontology refute the young Earth theory, and harmonize very well with an age of the Earth of around four and a half billion years. If we accept that the Earth is just a few thousand years old, we have to reject many different scientific conclusions, including age dating using radioactive carbon.

While the thesis of micro-evolution but not macro-evolution (CS-2), appears to have the status of a stipulation that cannot be false, a conflict arises between this contention and thesis (CS-3) of a world-wide flood around five thousand years ago. Based upon a conservative estimate of one million as the number of animal species known to exist today (Wilson 1992, p. 136), if there were twenty thousand animals aboard the Ark just five thousand years ago—or ten thousand sexually-reproducing species—then for a million species to exist today, around 990,000 new species must have evolved over the past five thousand years. And that, in turn, represents a rate of speciation of about two hundred new species a year! (The numbers depend on the precise dating of the flood and the exact number of sexually-reproducing species, but these figures are appropriate ballpark estimates.)

Given Noah's Flood, then either there are not at least one million known living animal species today or evolution has been taking place at the rate of about two hundred new species a year since the Flood! If there was a world-wide flood and the story of the Ark is true, then macro-evolution as well as micro-evolution has to have been taking place at the rate of approximately two hundred new species a year. Even if the young Earth theory (CS-1), is left to one side, the thesis of a world-wide flood (CS-3) contradicts the thesis of micro-evolution but not macro-evolution (CS-2), which in turn implies that Creation Science cannot possibly be true. Unless (CS-1) is associated with a specific age estimate, it is empirically untestable and therefore does not qualify as science. When it is associated with a specific age estimate, it turns out to empirically testable and demonstrably false. Even more consequentially, since the truth of (CS-3) contradicts the truth of (CS-2), Creation Science is an indefensible doctrine. It cannot possibly be true.

That a doctrine happens to be indefensible does not imply that no one is going to continue to believe it, since degrees of credibility (or credulousness) differ from person to person and from time to time. We are all more easily persuaded of some claims than we are of others because of our prior beliefs. The indefensibility of Creation Science should have an impact on those whose degrees of credibility tend to converge with degrees of rationality, or reasonableness, relative to justifiable standards of logic and the available relevant evidence. The difference is that credulousness, like gullibility, is a subjective property of each person, which can change across time, for example, with the acquisition of education and training. Reasonableness is defined on the basis of objective standards of logic that do not vary from person to person or from time to time. Persons tend to be reasonable to the extent to which their degrees of credibility satisfy objective standards.

Those who qualify as 'true believers' will have no difficulty rejecting the conclusion that Creation Science cannot possibly be sustained merely because the tenet of a world-wide flood five thousand years ago contradicts the tenet that micro- but not macro-evolution occurs, based upon very simple calculations of the number of species that were aboard the Ark and the number of species that exist today. The division of a one million species by five thousand years yields two hundred new species per year. But if you want to believe—sincerely want to believe!—that Creation Science is correct, nonetheless, then you can preserve your consistency by rejecting either the premise that there are now at least a million known living species or the premise that the world-wide flood took place about five thousand years ago! The second option is unlikely to yield the outcome that a true believer desires, however, since any number of known living species in excess of ten thousand would appear to produce the same dilemma—unless, of course, that figure of a million known living species represents micro-evolutionary variations upon the original ten thousand, in which case it might be possible to preserve consistency once again!

The discovery of previously unknown species, which continues unabated, would appear to undermine that alternative, no matter how appealing it may initially seem. A google search turns up report after report of the discovery of one new species after another: new species of fish, new species of shark, new species of honeyeater birds, new species of insects, news species of assassin spiders, new species of primate giant apes, new species of rorqual whales, new species of lemurs, new species of window bugs, new species of crab, even new species of carnivorous fairy shrimp! They range from new species of micro-organisms, like chlamydiae, *C. pneumoniae*, and *C. pecorum*, to vast numbers of new species of animals and plants in 'Lost Worlds' of New Guinea and Indonesia up to even more curious species that represent kinds of cross-species.

Among the most important finds, no doubt, are the new species of giant ape with characteristics of both gorillas and chimpanzees that has been sighted in the jungles north of Congo. These new giant apes grow up to six feet, five inches in height and weight between 187 and 224 pounds. They have large, black faces (like gorillas), consume a diet rich in fruit (like chimpanzees), and their males make nests on the ground (like gorillas) ("New' Giant Ape Found in DR Congo', BBC News, 10th October, 2004). Another fascinating find, this time in Indonesia, is the fossil of a new species of tiny humans, which may have lived as recently as thirteen thousand years ago. The species stood about three feet in height with a brain the size of a grapefruit ('Tiny Species of Human Unearthed', NewScientist.com, 27th October, 2004). The species has been designated *Homo floresiensis* and, from the artifacts that were found in caves near the discovery, used stone tools and ate bats, rats, and fish, which they cooked. According to the report, the caves also contained the bones and teeth of several dwarf stegondons, precursors of the modern elephant.

The very idea that there are only a fixed number of species dating from the Ark thus becomes increasingly difficult to maintain with the discovery of more and more new species, which steadily increase in their number across time. Thomas S. Kuhn (1962) has described the characteristics of conceptual schemes or 'paradigms' that are progressive when they lead to the integration of new hypotheses and evidence within a domain but that become degenerate when they are besieged by mounting 'anomalies' they cannot accommodate. Those who want to preserve the paradigm in the face of potential falsifiers treat the inconsistent evidence as though it were a puzzle to be solved instead of showing that the paradigm should be abandoned. Even Kuhn, who focuses upon the psychology of scientists as opposed to the logic of science, regards such an attitude as rational only so long as no better theory with more encompassing scope becomes available. Evolution appears to provide that more encompassing theory.

Creation Science thus appears to be a degenerating paradigm. While some may want to preserve it in the face of contradictory evidence, its tenability diminishes along with the accumulation of anomalies that it finds difficult to explain. The multiple causal mechanisms of evolutionary theory combined with descriptions of conditions that obtained at the time can provide historical explanations of their emergence that makes appeals to distinctions between 'micro' and 'macro'evolution unsustainable. Indeed, classic Creation Science texts, such as Walter Brown, *In the Beginning* (1995), depict micro-evolution as a horizontal process of variations within a species, whereas macro-evolution is a vertical process of new species emerging from earlier ones As his own illustration, new species of lizards, for example, may emerge as the products of micro-evolution from earlier species of lizards, but species of birds do not emerge as the products of macro-evolution from earlier species of lizard (Brown 1995, p. 6).

The discovery of a new species of dinosaur that was a feathered cousin of *T. Rex* may well qualify as the symbolic dagger in the heart of Creation Science as a theory. The discovery of this tiny dinosaur, which inhabited the lakeside forests of Liaoning Province in Northern China around 130 million years ago, confirmed predictions by paleontologists that a species of this very kind would eventually be discovered ('New Dinosaur Discovered: T. Rex Cousin Had Feathers', *National Geographic News*, 6th October, 2004). The new species, which has been named *Dilong paradoxus* (for its 'paradoxical' feathers), a five-foot long carnivore, had been predicted by Thomas Holtz, a vertebrate paleontologist from the University of Maryland. I suppose that, if a dedicated Creation Scientist wanted to insist that dinosaurs are not lizards and that Brown's illustration has therefore not been refuted, then it would make sense to observe that the evolution of birds from dinosaurs is an equally good refutation.

It turns out there have been earlier discoveries of links between birds and dinosaurs. Another species, *Sinovenator changii*, also discovered in the Liaoning Province of China, fills another gap in the evolutionary record. "This new dinosaur, which was probably feathered, is closely related to and almost the same age as the oldest known bird, *Archaeopteryx*," said Peter Makovicky, assistant curator of The Field Museum. "It demonstrates that major structural modifications toward birds occurred much earlier in the evolutionary process than was previously thought" ('New Species Clarifies Bird-Dinosaur Link', ScienceDaily.com, 14th February, 2002). In another article on this discovery, Makovicky observes, "These findings help counter, once and for all, the position of paleontologists who argue that birds did not evolve from dinosaurs" ('New Species Clarifies Bird-Dinosaur Link: Field Museum Paleontologist Helps Analyze Fossil', The Field Museum Information: Press Room, 2005). And it also helps counter, once and for all, the position of Creation Scientists who argue that only micro-evolution but not macro-evolution is possible.

# 3.1 *Why Intelligent Design Won't Do*

That Creation Science qualifies as a degenerating paradigm within the Kuhnian scheme of things has not dissuaded Christian fundamentalists from their desire to bring religion into the science classroom. Perhaps Freud could explain the determination with which this group has sought to force Biblical beliefs into the public schools, which bears the classic signs of an obsession: repeated, persistent, enduring and compulsive efforts using social, political, and legal avenues of approach, with the single-minded objective of introducing theistic alternatives to evolutionary theory into the science curriculum. And that, of course, is the rub. There may be a place for teaching religion in its multiple manifestations in the public schools, but there would appear to be virtually insuperable objections to misrepresenting religious doctrine as science.

From the perspective of this investigation, the Intelligent Design movement appears to abandon Creation Science and even classic creationism for a return to more traditional conceptions of the relationship between a creator and the world. The Intelligent Design approach is more abstract and less detailed than traditional creationist conceptions. Even the language of 'creator' as a synonymy for 'God' is abandoned in favor of the phrase 'Intelligent Design' and the conception of an Intelligent Designer. The movement maintains that there are organs and organisms in the world that display forms of complexity beyond the capacity of evolution to explain. Some of these exhibit what the proponents of Intelligent Design call 'irreducible complexity', where the displacement of any single part would cause the organ to cease to function, which is thus supposed to require an Intelligent Designer, since it could not have emerged by evolution.

That, at least, is the underlying claim. The foremost representative of this approach is Michael J. Behe, an associate professor of biochemistry at Lehigh. In his book, *Darwin's Black Box* (1996), Behe lays down the challenge to offer an account of bacterial flagella, for example, which are motor-like properties that enable bacteria to propel themselves by means of their rapid rotation. Another example—the favorite among those who favor this approach—is the human eye, a structure that seemingly defies explanation on the basis of the causal mechanisms of evolution. As a non-biological example of irreducible complexity, Behe offers a household mousetrap, with its unique arrangement of a platform, a hammer, a spring and a catch, with a holding bar. When the catch is moved, the holding bar releases the spring and the trap snaps shut.

From a logical point of view, the Intelligent Design movement depends on an argument by analogy for its plausibility. The Intelligent Designer is to the world as an artisan is to his artifacts. Or, at least, the Intelligent Designer is to the irreducibly complex elements of the world as an artisan is to his artifacts. The Intelligent Designer differs from the artisan insofar as an artisan, such as a woodworker, inhabits space and time and uses tools, such as planes, saws, and hammers, which have known and predictable causes and effects. People can apprentice to become woodworkers and learn to use tools such as planes, saws, and hammers. But what about the Intelligent Designer? Does he inhabit space and time? And what tools does he use? What are his 'planes, saws, and hammers'? Could anyone apprentice to become an Intelligent Designer?

That some of these questions sound at least faintly ridiculous suggests that the Intelligent Design movement may be based upon a faulty analogy. That, of course, would not be especially surprising, since comparisons between natural and supernatural phenomena tend to be problematic. Arguments by analogy compare one thing or kind of thing with another, contending that, since the first has properties A, B, C, and D, and the second has A, B, and C, for example, so the second should also have D. They are faulty when (a) there are more differences than similarities, (b) there are few but crucial differences, or (c) the argument is taken to be conclusive. That two things share certain traits in common, after all, provides inductive support that they may share another but not deductive proof.

From a historical point of view, Intelligent Design is old wine in new bottles as the latest incarnation of what is classically known as the Argument from Design. It was subjected to a devastating critique by David Hume in the eighteenth century. A perfect and complete Earth suggests a perfect and complete creator, while a finite and flawed Earth suggests a finite and flawed creator. Does anyone want to claim we have a perfect and complete Earth under any remotely plausible interpretation of that phrase? That suggests a finite and flawed creator. Who knows how many prototypes of Earth might have gone before and been discarded? Woodworkers frequently discard their flawed attempts at creating artifacts. Perhaps the world we inhabit might be among them. Who knows how many gods or goddesses may have been involved? Who knows how any of this could possibly have been done?

Comparisons between supernatural entities and natural entities are bound to involve more differences than similarities, no matter what we call them. If we cannot know whether god is one or many, how many gods there might be or even whether god is male or female, then calling God 'the Intelligent Designer' is not likely to enhance our understanding. We are as ignorant about any presumptive Intelligent Designer as we are of any 'God'—with the possible difference that, as long as we take our analogy seriously, we are impaled by the properties of human artisans as evidence of the properties of an Intelligent Designer. Since we know the tools and practices that woodworkers employ to make their artifacts, isn't it a crucial dissimilarity that we don't know the tools and practices Intelligent Designers use to produce their artifacts? Indeed, we don't even know how many of these Designers there may be!

The mousetrap as an example of irreducible complexity, moreover, suggests that the comparison between products of cultural evolution and the products of genetic evolution requires further contemplation. Thoughtful humans think things through, they reason and experiment, create prototypes and analyze them. The Intelligent Designer might well be expected to perform all of these tasks, on the assumption, of course, that he, she, or it has the capacity to think things through, to reason and experiment, create prototypes and analyze them. The point is that we really have no idea how any of these things could possibly be done by an entity beyond space and time of which we appear to have no knowledge. Human thought processes take place within human brains. Are we to assume, on the basis of another analogy, that the Intelligent Designer also has a mind and, if so, that it takes place within the Designer's brain? And where is that located?

The idea of 'building a better mousetrap' suggests the possibility of trial and error learning and of learning from experience. Is that a trait that we would be inclined to attribute to an Intelligent Designer? After all, humans are intelligent, but their degrees of intelligence vary widely. Just how intelligent is this Designer supposed to be? Is there any way we could tell, or is this just a belief that many of us want to adopt because it makes us feel more secure in a world that is full of threats and promises, where threats tend to predominate? And if there is more than one Intelligent Designer, could it be that the world is the product of a committee? And if we reason from what we know about committees in our own true life experience, is there any reason to have confidence that the product of Intelligent Design is going to be intelligent on any reasonable interpretation of its meaning? Just how seriously are we supposed to take the implied analogy?

Reasoning by analogy is frequently flawed and does not invariably qualify as scientific. In the absence of objective standards, what qualifies as an adequate answer to a question tends to vary from person to person and from time to time. Subjective certitude is not the same as scientific adequacy. The aim of science, as we know, is the discovery of laws of nature, including the laws of physics, the laws of chemistry and the laws of biology. These laws are the foundation of scientific explanations, predictions, and retrodictions. If it is a law that water freezes at thirty-two degrees Fahrenheit, then together with suitable information about initial conditions, it provides a premise for predicting that, when water reaches that temperature, it will freeze, and when it does freeze, together with information that the temperature hit thirty-two degrees, can explain why. But their conditions of adequacy are specifiable.

Those conditions include requirements of derivability, lawlikeness, and exclusion of irrelevant factors. Unless we know the means by which one or more Intelligent Designers brings about their effects, how could we possibly subject them to suitable empirical tests? And if we can't subject them to suitable empirical tests, how can any hypothesis of this general kind qualify as scientific? And if it cannot qualify as scientific, then what is the basis for its inclusion in the science curriculum of a public school? These are ideas that can be taught and discussed in churches and in synagogues, in temples and in mosques, where the scientific standing of ideas may not matter very much. Why, then, should so much insistence be placed upon the inclusion of hypotheses like Intelligent Design in a public school science curriculum when they do not qualify as scientific? What is the rationale for including them?

Even Behe admits that there are earlier versions of mousetraps, which suggests in turn that there may be earlier versions of human eyes. The complexity of the human eye invites explanation on the basis of the laws of biology together with information about the specific conditions that have occurred during the course of natural history. These laws include a set of at least eight causal mechanisms—not only genetic mutation and natural selection, as some creation scientists have said, but genetic drift, sexual reproduction, sexual selection, group selection, artificial selection, and genetic engineering. As we have already discovered, four enhance genetic diversity and four determine which genes are perpetuated through time. Is it impossible to explanation the evolution of the human eye by invoking them?

Suppose, for example, that a kind of black algae had acquired land motility and a single light-sensitive cell. If that sensitivity to light was remotely advantageous in adapting to the environment by promoting sensitivity to locations that happen to be even slightly more nutrient-rich than alternative locations, for example, it is rather easy to imagine that mutations of additional light-sensitive cells in various formations could rapidly evolve as an effect of natural selection. Over millions of years, the result might look like the product of Intelligent Design, but it would be the outcome of purely causal processes. Indeed, the point of evolutionary theory is to explain the origin of species without having to make any appeal to intelligence or to divine design. That was Darwin's purpose: to provide a natural explanation for phenomena that give the appearance of being the result of Intelligent Design!

It's not as though evolutionary biologists have been unaware of the problem of accounting for the evolution of complexity. Behe's book includes references to William Jennings Bryan, for example, but not to John Tyler Bonner. Yet it is Bonner, not Bryan, who has devoted himself to the study of this problem. One of the most important, if not the most important, studies within this domain is his *The Evolution of Complexity by Means of Natural Selection* (1988). It's a bit puzzling that Behe, who professes profound interest in the evolution of complexity, does not even acknowledge the existence of the work of the leading scholar who deals with the evolution of complexity!

When it comes to the scientific explanation of phenotypes and geno-types, the causal mechanisms of evolution have no real competition. We know that different theories of evolution appeal to different combinations of these mechanisms, where accounting for the evolution of species appears to require invoking them all. That the human species has evolved from ear-lier species has becomes apparent from the discovery of our many ances-tors, including *Australopithecus*, Java Man, Peking Man, Neanderthal Man, and Cro-Magnon Man. And only evolution has the capacity to account for them. Appeals to God or to an Intelligent Designer explain nothing. How many acts of special creation would all of this have required? More impor-tantly, exactly how is any of this supposed to have been done?

We also know that we share more than ninety-eight percent of our genes with chimpanzees. This may not guarantee that we  share common ancestors, but it is powerful evidence that points in that direction. Small differences in genes can make considerable differences in their manifesta-tions, especially in view of the influence of pleiotropic and polygenic effects, where single genes affect multiple traits or combinations of genes affect single traits. Once the role of pleiotropic and polygenic effects is properly understood, it's very difficult not to recognize that there do not have to be 'missing links' that fill every gap between different species. Nature can experiment and discover which combinations work and which do not on the basis of very small differences in genes that can have very great differences in phenotypes. Some 'links' are not 'missing'.

How do DNA and skeletal similarities between species, for example, figure in the grand design? An Intelligent Designer could have created new arrangements for different species, yet there are underlying similarities in the skeletal structures of lizards, dinosaurs, birds, and human beings. Doesn't all of this suggest the operation of the causal mechanisms of evolution of long duration rather than repeated acts of special creation? Morphological similarities, DNA comparisons, the fossil record and geological evidence support the general conception of an Earth that is about 4.5 billion years old, where life emerged around six hundred million years ago and humanoid life around five million years ago. Appeals to an unknowable source using unspecified means does nothing to fill the gaps in our knowledge. It merely substitutes pretense for what we don't know, ignorance that in the past has proven to be temporary.

## 3.2  *Bad Arguments for Intelligent Design*

For the hypothesis of Intelligent Design to be taken seriously as a scientific theory, it would have to possess predictive as well as explanatory significance. Without knowledge of the causal mechanisms used by the Intelligent Designer, it is not a testable theory, because it cannot pass conditions of derivability and of lawlikeness. What are the laws that were used in designing the world and its specific features? With knowledge of those causal mechanisms, however, there is no need to invoke the Designer itself. The situation parallels that of classic Creationist hypothesis (CC-3), as I explain in the Appendix. Either way, there is no place in science for the Intelligent Designer hypothesis. It cannot satisfy conditions of adequacy (CA-1) and (CA-2), on the one hand, and even if it could, it would be unable to satisfy the condition for the exclusion of explanatorily irrelevant factors, (CA-3), on the other.

Bad arguments for Intelligent Design are multiplying rapidly. A recent column in a local paper by Intelligent Design advocate Jeff Marino (*Duluth News Tribune*, 19th March, 2005) offers a nice example. Jeff defines 'science' as restricted to what can be observed and subject to experiment by means of repeatable units within a three-dimensional world. If God (or the Intelligent Designer) is unobservable or outside of our three-dimensional world, then the God hypothesis cannot qualify as scientific. But God is both. So his own definition disqualifies his own hypothesis as science. It may be unusual to discover that an argument has the qualify of being self-refuting, but this appears to be an illustration. Even if Jeff were right, he would still be wrong.

Science is not restricted to what can be observed, but it must be possible to derive some consequences from hypotheses that are capable of being tested, under appropriate conditions, by means of observation, measurement, or experiment. The basic flaw, in fact, is not that God is unobservable but that God hypotheses have no observable, measurable, or experimental consequences for us to test. Marino also insists that evolution violates natural laws, which would be a fascinating and even devastating result, if it were true. The several examples he offers, which are either mistaken or wrong, are nonetheless instructive in reviewing attempts to defend the indefensible.

Marino's first example he calls "the law of cause and effect," namely: that every effect must have a cause. Calling this a law does not make it one, however, and this is simply a definitional truth. An event only qualifies as 'an effect' because it has 'a cause'. So if an event ever occurs without any cause, we could not call this event 'an effect'. He then asks, 'Where did the original matter and energy come from?' Notice this is a question about cosmology, not evolution. It might be taken as asking, 'Why is there something rather than nothing?', which I am willing to grant is a question for which there appears to be no scientific answer. However, if he means, as in the case of the First Cause and Prime Mover arguments for the existence of God, that there had to be a first cause or a prime mover to initiate the world's history, it appears rooted in the religious belief that the world had to have a beginning in time.

No doubt most of us tend to take for granted that the origin of the universe had to be unique and unrepeatable. The presumption that the world had to have a beginning in time, however, as the Preface explains, turns out to be indefensible on logical and on physical grounds. The sequence of positive and negative integers from zero up and zero down illustrates a numerical sequence that has no beginning and no end. So the idea of a sequence having no beginning and no end is at least logically possible. And, indeed, on both Steady State and Big Bang models, it also seems physically possible. On Steady State models, the universe has always existed and always will exist with a globally uniform, locally varied distribution of matter and energy. It has no beginning.

On Big Bang models, the universe began with an explosion creating photons and neutrinos from electrons and protons, but cooled sufficiently for electrons to join nuclei and form atoms of hydrogen and helium, which condensed to form galaxies and stars and eventually Earth. If the universe continues to expand until there is a completely homogenous distribution of matter and energy, it ends with 'a whimper'. Depending upon its exact mass, however, it may reach a point at which the influence of gravity takes over, contracting matter and energy back together in a Big Crunch. Given that scenario, we could be in one of an endless series of cycles of Big Bang-expansion-contraction-Big Crunch, where there is no first and no last historical world. In this case, too, there is no need for God as a First Cause because there is no beginning and there is no end.

Each specific initiation of a cycle in an endlessly recycling series of 'big bangs' could not qualify as science if its manifestations were incapable of observation, measurement, or experimentation. Even though each of those initiations is unique and unrepeatable as a singular event, it remains testable as an event of a specific kind. The detectable effects of 'big bangs' thus include the recession of distant galaxies and weak radio static that fills the universe, which have been found by astronomical observation. An analysis of the early stages of the big bang are the subject of a very accessible book by Stephen Weinberg, *The First Three Minutes* (1977), whose author would be awarded the Nobel Prize in 1979. While we do not have direct access to big bangs, including our own, their occurrence, nevertheless, can still be tested based on their empirical effects.

Marino calls his second example 'the law of biogenesis', which states that life only comes from life. But this is no more a natural law than the first. It exemplifies the classic fallacy known as 'begging the question', in which you assume as a premise what must be established on independent grounds. Deriving a conclusion from itself as an assumed premise, after all, is deductively valid. But that does not make such claims true! Scientists are actively investigating the conditions that are specific to the origin of life on Earth as it cooled, including water vapor and carbonic gases. Retroviruses may hold the key. The mystery is unresolved, but science is making progress. And it ought to be apparent that, however satisfying it may be subjectively, appealing to God (or to an Intelligent Designer) to plug this gap makes no contribution to scientific knowledge.

Science proceeds by a process of successive approximation, where hypotheses and theories that account for and explain the available evidence at one time may require revision or rejection as more evidence becomes available. There will always be gaps in what we know about the world around us. The critical consideration, here and elsewhere, is that filling gaps by appeals to an unknowable source using unspecified means is merely the substitution of one kind of ignorance for another. A sense of psychological certainty is a poor substitute for an objective explanation. It cannot satisfy any of the conditions of derivability, lawlikeness, or exclusion of irrelevant factors.

Marino's third example is the second law of thermodynamics, which, he says, dictates that matter and energy go from states of higher order and complexity to states of lower. This example is a *bona fide* law, but he over-looks that it is a statistical law describing the behavior of systems on the average. Systems that tend toward the dissipation of energy globally are still consistent with the emergence of greater complexity locally, which reconciles biology with physics, as we have already discovered. Systems that are reversible, such as recycling 'big bang' sequences, go both ways. Thus, when it is properly understood, even the second law of thermody-namics poses no obstacles to reconciling physics with biology. Neither Creation Science nor Intelligent Design are able to derive support from the laws of physics, which are compatible with biology.

While Marino also offers quotes from famous biologists who admit our knowledge is incomplete, those do not qualify as endorsements of Intelligent Design. Those who understand the role of polygenic and pleiotropic effects, where many genes influence the development of single traits and single genes influence the development of many traits, recog-nize that transitions between organisms and species need not be smooth or continuous, but can exhibit striking differences and discontinuities, which could result from the alteration of even a single gene. No matter how many new fossils or so-called 'missing links' science may discover, creationists can always claim that there should be more. But that would be justifiable only if evolution has to be gradual and continuous, when it can be intermittent and gappy. Some gaps are the way things are!

The most misleading ingredient of Marino's position, however, is his claim that evolution asserts upward progression "by chance." He acknowl-edges none of the eight causal mechanisms of evolution, including genetic mutation, natural selection, sexual reproduction, genetic drift, sexual selection, group selection, artificial selection, and genetic engineer-ing. These mechanisms are the lawful basis for evolutionary science that make its hypotheses both explanatory and testable and, in relation to par-ticular historical conditions, predictive as well. This is roughly on a par with Walter Brown's claim that evolution is a theory without a mecha-nism, which he contradicted when he further asserted that its only mech-anisms are genetic mutations and natural selection.

The foundation for Marino's position on "chance" may be found in arguments presented by other proponents of Intelligent Design. An inter-esting paper by Reverend Bill McGinnis (entitled, 'Intelligent Design Can Be Tested Scientifically', LoveAllPeople.com), correctly remarks that Intelligent Design is a concept of religion or of philosophy rather than of science. He offers the fascinating suggestion that, insofar as the world is the product of Intelligent Design, it is the obligation of Science to under-stand its results:

Science is only a means to understanding that which was created by
Intelligent Design . . . where it is not the responsibility of Intelligent
Design to follow the methods of Science, but the responsibility of Science
to understand and explain that which was created by Intelligent Design.

This question-begging declaration deserves no comment, but it's worth
looking at an argument McGinnis presents, based upon statistical
probabilities.

According to McGinnis, if we ascribe statistical probabilities—which
he does not otherwise define—to "the earth itself, with its perfect atmos-
phere to sustain life; perfect temperature for life; perfect cycle of night
and day; perfect cycle of seasons; perfect soil for growing crops; fish to eat
in the rivers and oceans; animals to eat on earth; perfect amount of water
for drinking," and so forth, then we will discover that, for all of these
properties to have come together at the same time by chance is "about one
in a million zillion," drawing the conclusion. "So even if we do not consider the staggering complexity of biological life, it is statistically impossible that our earth simply happened by chance, or by any imagined
combination of pre-existing natural processes."

The argument suffers from serious flaws. First, his conclusion tacitly
shifts from overwhelming improbability ("about one in a million zillion") to what he calls "statistical impossibility," which does not follow.
Events that are extremely improbable are not therefore impossible, yet
his use of 'statistical impossibility' is sufficiently ambiguous to take in the
unwary. Second, like Marino, McGinnis ignores the eight causal mechanisms of evolution—genetic mutation, natural selection, sexual reproduction, genetic drift, sexual selection, group selection, artificial
selection, and genetic engineering—which produce outcomes that are
not the products of chance; at least, they are not the products of chance
as coincidental or accidental happenings. Third, he appears unable to
appreciate that the actual must be possible, where, since we have evolved
on Earth, that must have been possible, no matter how improbable.
Unless the conditions for life and evolution had been favorable, we
would not be here.

A striking feature of this argument is that it ignores calculations
intended to supply estimates of the possible existence of other species
throughout the universe. What is called the 'Drake equation', for example,
adopts educated guesses about the average rate of star formation, R,
which is assigned the value 10; the fraction of stars that could contain
planetary systems, *fp*, which is assigned the value of .1; the number of
planets per star that are Earthlike, *ne*, which is assigned the value of 1; the

fraction of Earthlike planets upon which life could develop, $fl$, which is also assigned the value of 1. Since our galaxy, the Milky Way, contains around a hundred billion stars, there would appear to be ample opportunities for life to have developed elsewhere in the universe (White 1999, Chapter 2), which completely undermines this line of argument.

An influential variation has been advanced by William A. Dembski, who has been a research professor in the conceptual foundations of science at Baylor University. As H. Allen Orr has observed ('Devolution: Why Intelligent Design Isn't', *The New Yorker*, 30th May, 2005), Dembski suggests that complex objects must be the result of intelligence if they are the products neither of chance nor of necessity. So Dembski broadens the alternatives from 'chance versus intelligence' (McGinnis) to 'chance versus necessity versus intelligence' (Dembski). The kind of necessity he has in mind, presumably, is physical necessity, which occurs when effects are brought about by initial conditions and natural laws. But there's a hidden ambiguity here as well, since laws of nature can be deterministic or indeterministic, as we saw earlier. Deterministic laws are those for which same cause–same effect always obtains, while indeterministic laws are those where same cause–same probable effects obtain.

Since evolution in accordance with laws of either kind would govern outcomes that occur by necessity, as long as its effects are brought about by initial conditions and natural laws, there is nothing involved here that dictates a role for intelligence. We have already found it is a mistake to regard the effects of the eight causal mechanisms of evolution as matters of chance in the sense that matters here—even as indeterministic causal processes—because their outcomes are not merely the results of coincidence or accident. We're left with an apparent choice between necessity and intelligence. But what occurs by law happens by necessity in the appropriate sense. So nothing about the origin of species dictates that intelligence must play a role. Demski only makes a case for intelligence by treating chance as coincidence and necessity as determinism. Absent those question-begging assumptions, his conclusion does not follow. And this means that the theory of Intelligent Design remains in search of an intelligent defense.

## 3.3 *Intelligent Design before the Court of Law.*

The intellectual shortcomings of the theory of Intelligent Design has not inhibited Christian fundamentalists from advancing it as a candidate for inclusion in public school systems in many parts of the country. They have insisted that it be taught as part of the science curriculum, which raises serious questions about its standing.

As we have seen, Intelligent Design is not a scientific hypothesis and therefore does not belong in the science curriculum. But philosophical analysis and political actions are disparate activities, where one does not often constrain the other. Some school boards have moved to have it included in their public school science curriculum, which, when challenged, has moved the controversy from the domain of intellectual inquiry into the public courts of law.

The case that captivated the nation involved the decision by the Dover Area School District of Pennsylvania, which, in October 2004, declared that, beginning in January 2005, Intelligent Design would be included in the ninth-grade biology curriculum. A group of parents affected by the decision filed a suit alleging that this decision was an effort to establish religion in violation of the First Amendment of the Constitution, which guarantees not only freedom of speech and of the press but freedom of religion. The case was decided in December 2005 by Judge John Jones, who handed down a 139-page decision exploring both legal and intellectual dimensions of the case (Jones 2005). A summary overview has been published by Jason Rosenhouse (Rosenhouse 2006), but here I want to examine the foundation for the decision to exclude Intelligent Design from the biology curriculum in Dover.

In his decision, the judge observes that Christian fundamentalism arose in the nineteenth century as a response to social changes, new religious thinking, and the advent of Darwinism as a naturalistic explanation of the origin of species on the basis of natural selection. Motivated by religious concerns, various groups attempted to influence their state legislatures to restrict instruction in evolution as part of the public school curriculum, culminating in the criminal prosecution in 1927 of a public school teacher named John T. Scopes in Tennessee, where the judge excluded expert scientific testimony from the defense. Pitting two of the nation's greatest orators, Clarence Darrow for the defense and William Jennings Bryan for the prosecution, the case created a sensation. While Scopes was found guilty of teaching evolution in violation of a Tennessee law and assessed a $100 fine, the state was widely ridiculed for having 'monkey laws' (Berra 1990, Chapter 5).

The next major decision occurred in 1968, when the Supreme Court ruled that an Arkansas law prohibiting the teaching of evolution was unconstitutional. The proponents of Biblical views then promoted 'balanced treatment' legislation that granted equal-time to religious and to non-religious viewpoints, but that approach was found to be in violation of federal law in 1975. This outcome eventually lead those who wanted to promote a return to 'fundamentals' and their instruction in the classroom to adopt another tactic by offering scientific-sounding language for thinly-disguised Biblical accounts of the origin of life in the form of Creation Science, including the doctrines of a young-Earth, of a world-wide flood, and of the non-emergence of new species from previously existing species. The rationale, no doubt, was in the spirit of the adage, 'If you can't lick 'em, join 'em'!

In an important decision in 1987, however, the Supreme Court ruled that the Establishment Clause against the establishment of government-sponsored religion was violated by teaching Creation Science, which turned the Appeals Court ruling of 1975 into national policy. According to that clause, "Congress shall make no law respecting an establishment of religion, or prohibiting the free exercise thereof," an injunction extended to the states by the Fourteenth Amendment. The appropriate standard for determining whether the Dover policy is Constitutional, as both sides agreed, was set forth in a 1971 decision known as 'the Lemon test', according to which a policy or practice is unconstitutional if the defendant's primary purpose is to advance religion or the adoption of the School Board's new policy had the primary effect of advancing religion. The Court found that it failed this standard.

An important part of the evidence on which the Court rendered its verdict was testimony that the members of the School Board had not only acknowledged that they wanted to put religion back into the schools but that they had manipulated the science curriculum by threatening to withhold funding for a biology textbook unless another book entitled *Of Pandas and People* (1993) was also made available to students in their biology course. There was ample testimony that the members of the Board had more or less consciously, through their deliberations, decided to substitute the words 'Intelligent Design' for the word 'Creationism'. Not only was there legal proof that the Board's motivation was primarily religious but the judge found that its members repeatedly lied about their purpose in embracing *Pandas* and in adopting policies that had the effect of the endorsement of a specific faith.

The history of the Board's decisions leaves scant room for doubt on the purpose for its actions. On 18th October 2004, by 6–3, it adopted the following resolution:

> Students will be made aware of gaps/problems in Darwin's theory and of other theories of evolution including, but not limited to, intelligent design. Note: Origins of Life is not taught.

Presumably, what is meant by this brief passage is that students will be made aware of gaps or problems in Darwin's theory and made aware of other theories of evolution including, but not limited to, Intelligent Design. It does not state that the students will be made aware of gaps or problems with these alternative theories, including Intelligent Design, perhaps the most important of which is whether Intelligent Design properly qualifies as a *scientific* theory.

The Board mandated that, commencing in January 2005, ninth-grade biology teachers would be required to read a four-paragraph statement singling out evolution as a subject in which instruction and standardized tests are required by the state. It included three more paragraphs, the first of which is as follows:

> Because Darwin's Theory is a theory, it continues to be tested as new evidence is discovered. The Theory is not a fact. Gaps in the theory exist for which there is no evidence. A theory is defined as a well-tested explanation that unifies a broad range of observations.

This was not the original wording proposed by the teachers, acting under duress, who had suggested that Darwin's theory ought to be described as "the dominant scientific theory," which the Board edited out. The teachers also had included the word "yet," so that the third sentence would have read, "Gaps in the theory exist for which there is yet no evidence." The observation that there is "a significant amount of evidence" supporting the theory was also proposed but not included.

From a philosophical point of view, the first paragraph appears more or less innocuous. The term 'fact' can be construed either as having the same meaning as 'truth'—in which case, the sentence, "The Theory is not a fact," presumably, is intended to assert that it isn't true—or as having the same meaning as 'proven true'—in which case, the sentence, "The Theory is not a fact," presumably, asserts that it has not been proven to be true. Since the last sentence defines "a theory" as "a well-tested explanation that unifies a broad range of observations," putting the first sentence together with the last yields the claim that Darwin's theory is a well-tested explanation that unifies a broad range of observations, albeit one that, on the more charitable interpretation of the text, has not been proven to be true.

Although the teachers' recommendations would have made this paragraph a bit stronger and more accurate, there is not a lot to fault here, notwithstanding the suspicion that the Board would have liked to have used a weaker definition, according to which a theory is merely a speculation, conjecture, or guess. There is yet another sense that defines a theory is an empirically-testable explanatory hypothesis, whether or not it has ever actually been tested. Since a theory cannot have been 'well-tested' without being 'testable', however, apart from ambiguity about the meaning of 'fact', this first paragraph does not raise serious problems for scientific theories. It does, however, raise potentially serious problems for an alternative that is not well-tested or does not unify a broad range of observations. The Board may not have recognized that its own standard could defeat its purpose.

The second paragraph, by comparison, offers a description of Intelligent Design that raises more serious questions. The full text of that paragraph reads as follows:

> Intelligent Design is an explanation of the origin of life that differs from Darwin's view. The reference book, *Of Pandas and People*, is available for students who might be interested in gaining an understanding of what Intelligent Design actually involves.

Neither Intelligent Design nor Darwin's theory are primarily explanations of the origin of life. Darwin's theory tries to explain how life could have evolved from simple beginnings, and Intelligent Design tries to explain the origin of properties of living things that display 'irreducible complexity'.

The use of the term 'explanation', absent the qualification 'scientific', equivocates between the weak sense of a subjectively satisfying account and the far stronger sense of an adequate scientific explanation. The former, after all, might or might not be able to fulfill conditions of derivability, lawlikeness, and the exclusion of irrelevant factors imposed by the latter. Insofar as our previous discussion has found that the tenets of Creation Science are either empirically untestable or seem to be false, it runs the risk of being unable to qualify as 'a well-tested explanation that unifies a broad range of observations' and therefore of not qualifying as science.

The third paragraph may not initially appear to be important, since it suggests that biology students should "keep an open mind." Here is the language it used:

> With respect to any theory, students are encouraged to keep an open mind. The school leaves the discussion of the Origins of Life to individual students and their families. As a Standards-driven district, class instruction focuses upon preparing students to achieve proficiency on Standards-based assessments.

The Court would hear evidence that, while ostensibly encouraging their students to 'keep an open mind', the only alternative offered to evolution is not scientific but religious in the form of Intelligent Design; that by encouraging their students to discuss this with their parents, students can reasonable infer that the District's attitude is religious; and that this admonition thereby protects the alternative to evolution from critical scrutiny, which was perceived as threatening by the Board.

Serious problems developed during the trial about the scientific accuracy of the Board's preferred text. The only expert on paleontology, for example, testified that *Pandas* systematically distorted and misrepresented important tenets of evolution, including cladistics (the classification scheme for biological species), homology (the comparison of parts between organisms of various species), and exaptation (where a structure that served one function could change across time). Exaptation is very important in evolutionary theory, because, as in the case of the fins of fish evolving into fingers and bones and legs and toes for land-mobile animals, it is a mechanism for the emergence of new species from old, reflecting macro-evolution as a kind of micro-evolution across time. Other testimony similarly established that *Pandas* distorts or misrepresents evidence in the fossil record about pre-Cambrian fossils, the evolution of fish to amphibians, the evolution of small carnivorous dinosaurs into birds, the evolution of the mammalian middle ear, and the evolution of whales from land animals. Even the most important witness for Intelligent Design, Michael Behe, admitted that *Pandas* misinforms its readers about basic features of standard evolutionary theory.

Expert testimony during the trial supported the conclusions that the purported arguments for Intelligent Design do not satisfy the conception of scientific theories as testable hypotheses based upon natural explanations. As the opinion remarks,

> ID is reliant upon forces acting outside of the natural world, forces that we cannot see, replicate, control or test, which have produced changes in this world. While we [the Court] take no position on whether such forces exist, they are simply not testable by scientific means and therefore cannot qualify as part of the scientific process or as a scientific theory.

Indeed, three witnesses for the defense, including Behe, testified that, in order for Intelligent Design to satisfy the conditions that are requirements to qualify as science, it would be necessary to 'change the ground rules' or otherwise 'broaden the definition' to allow consideration of supernatural forces to qualify as science.

Even Behe's definition of 'irreducible complexity' turns out to suffer from what appears to be a fatal defect. Expert witnesses not only testified that his concept depends upon overlooking or ignoring established mechanisms of evolution but that his conception, according to which a system is 'irreducibly complex' when a precursor 'missing a part' is by definition *nonfunctional*, what he should mean is that a precursor 'missing a part' would function differently that it would when the part is present. This could even be said of the bacterial flagella, which might not function as a rotary motor when parts are missing but might instead serve another function, such as that of a secretory system, which, given the phenomena of exaptation, means that Behe's approach no longer has force in criticizing evolution.

Indeed, another expert testified that the evolution of the mammalian middle ear from a jaw bone as an example of exaptation was a transition in functions of parts across time that would be impossible, by definition, on Behe's conception. This resonates with the contention by Creation Scientists that micro-evolution, but not macro-evolution, is possible, as though it were a matter that could be settled by stipulation. In both cases, the evidence of evolution contradicts the prohibition against exaptation (by Behe) and the constraint on macro-evolution (by creation scientists). Questions about the origin of life and the evolution of species are empirical questions and cannot be answered simply by stipulation!

Although the Defendants persistently asserted that instruction on Intelligent Design was instituted in order to improve science education and encourage the exercise of critical thinking, the Court was not impressed. It found that none of the actions to be expected, if that was the Board's purpose, were pursued, such as consulting scientific publications, contacting scientific organizations, or even soliciting the advice of the District's own science teachers. On the contrary, the Board acted on the basis of legal advice from two organizations with dedicated religious, cultural, and legal commitments. Most of the members of the Board admitted that they had no clear understanding of Intelligent Design as a hypothesis or theory, which undermined the credibility of the defense position. The Court concluded the professed secular purposes were insincere and a sham.

Among the indicators the Court cited as evidence that Intelligent Design is not a scientific theory were that studies of Intelligent Design have not been published in peer-reviewed journals, it has failed to generate a research program devoted to developing and testing the theory it represents, and it has not gained adherents in the scientific community. Thus, the application of the Endorsement and the Lemon tests to the actions by the Dover School Board demonstrated to the Court that the Board's policy on Intelligent Design violates the Establishment clause and does not qualify as constitutional. "Our conclusion today is that it is unconstitutional to teach ID as an alternative to evolution in a public school science classroom," the court ruled.

One of the most fascinating aspects of the case emerged in the form of what the Court described as a "contrived dualism" advanced by Creation Scientists and by Christian fundamentalists that "one must either accept the literal interpretation of Genesis or else believe in the godless systems of evolution." On this approach, any problems with evolution count as evidence for Creationism. This might better be described as a 'specious bifurcation', which divides an issue along lines that are not theoretically justifiable and treats them as definitive. The Roman Catholic Church, for example, reconciles science and religion by adopting the position that God created the world and various forms of life using evolution. God could have used any means he wanted to create the world and forms of life, but those that he chose were the mechanisms of evolution. This combines evolution with theism.

The Court's decision was exceptionally clear and direct on this point. According to the judge, a common misconception underlies much support for their position: Both defendants and many of the leading proponents of ID make a bedrock assumption which is utterly false. Their presupposition is that evolutionary theory is antithetical to a belief in the existence of a supreme being and to religion in general. Repeatedly in this trial, the plaintiffs' scientific experts testified that the theory of evolution represents good science, that it is overwhelmingly accepted by the scientific community, and that it in no way conflicts with, nor does it deny, the existence of a divine Creator. It may be this false presupposition that drives think tanks, such as the Discovery Institute, to advocate the "defeat of scientific materialism and its destructive moral, cultural, and political legacies" and attempt to "replace materialistic explanations with the theistic understanding that nature and human beings are created by God." While some forms of materialism may be antithetical to belief in supreme beings, there is nothing about evolution as such that implies those forms of materialism.

Thus, if the eight causal mechanisms of evolution are adequate to explain and to predict the course of evolution relative to information about particular events during the world's history, then those laws belong in the science curriculum. But not the appeal to God, a hypothesis that does not qualify as scientific. It would not be inappropriate, however, to include the Intelligent Design hypothesis along with multiple other views about the origin of life in courses dealing with religious beliefs. A great deal of provincialism, bigotry, and intolerance are associated with fundamentalism in America. Courses in cultural anthropology and in comparative religions would have an enlightening effect and provide our students with a far broader education. But we should not substitute ideology for evolution. Render unto God that which is God's but also render unto Darwin that which is Darwin's.

# CHAPTER 4

# The Immorality of the Christian Right

➤ *We rely on our beliefs to guide our actions*

➤ *We're morally entitled to hold a belief only if we're logically entitled to hold it*

➤ *Of eight commonly-held moral theories, only one, treating other persons as ends-in-themselves, is defensible*

➤ *Persons acquire rights in graduated stages; stem cells, zygotes, embryos, or early-term fetuses are not persons*

➤ *It's immoral for religious persons to interfere politically with abortions, stem-cell research, or cloning*

$\mathcal{W}$e act on our beliefs. When our beliefs are true, our actions are, in those respects, appropriately guided. Whey they are false, they are, in those respects, inappropriate and misguided. A pragmatic conception of truth maintains that beliefs are true to the extent to which they provide appropriate guidance for action (Fetzer 1990). Truth, like directions themselves, is therefore amenable to degrees, where, relative to our objectives and goals, the more appropriate the guidance beliefs provide, the greater their truth. Truth may also be identified with correspondence to reality or, more broadly, with the way things are, a far more traditional conception, which explains why truths, which correspond with reality, provide appropriate guidance for actions.

Because we act on our beliefs, beliefs have causal consequences in the world that go beyond their merely logical implications. If we believe that abortion is murder, for example, and that doctors who perform them are 'baby killers', we may be disposed to take matters into our own hands and kill the killers of the innocent unborn—in the name of 'life'. Just as our actions must be moral to be worthy of praise rather than of condemnation, however, so too must our beliefs be worthy of acceptance rather than of rejection or—which for many may be far more difficult— suspension of belief. According to a principle known as *the ethics of belief* (Clifford 1879), we are morally entitled to hold a belief only when we are logically entitled to hold that belief. This principle sounds simple, but its effects can be profound.

An alternative approach known as *the will to believe* (James 1897) holds that in some cases a belief may be worthy of acceptance even if there is no empirical evidence in its support, especially when the causal consequences of adopting that belief are beneficial. Belief in God might be said to be justified because it makes a contribution to morality. The enormous differences in beliefs represented by the world's religions, however, not to mention the diverse sects and creeds of varied faiths, suggests that 'the will to believe' can take many and varied forms. It does not appear promising for resolving conflicts between members of diverse faiths.

The things we believe are things we take to be true. Those things we believe without evidence or contrary to evidence are articles of faith. Some of the beliefs upon which we act, moreover, may affect our behavior in a manner that exceeds normal expectations for human interaction. Many of our beliefs are supportable on the basis of the available evidence, but others go far beyond what could be established on the basis of observations, measurements, or experiments. And that includes most of our religious beliefs. Consider the following examples:

(E1)  Suicide bombers are recruited from Palestinian youth by Hamas partly by appealing to the promise, derived from the Quran, that, in return for martyrdom, not only will their families be financially compensated but they personally will have unlimited sex with seventy-two virgins in heaven. According to one young Muslim, Bassim Khalifi, sixteen, it has a powerful effect: "The boys can't stop thinking about the virgins" ('Devotion, Desire Spur Youths to Martyrdom', *USA Today*, 26th June, 2001);

(E2)  Three men in Sungai Siput, 130 miles north of Kuala Lumpur, Malaysia, were recently charged with capital murder in the killing of a woman from Duluth, Minnesota, during the course of "an alleged ritual sacrifice to obtain lottery numbers from the spirits." The body of the woman, Carolyn Janis Noriani Ahmad, "was discovered in a shallow grave at an oil palm plantation last month. She had been missing for nineteen months" ('Three Accused of Ritual Murder', *Duluth News Tribune*, 28th July, 2001); and,

(E3)  According to a very recent survey of religious opinions, thirty-six percent of Americans believe that the Book of Revelation contains "true prophecy"; fifty-five percent believe that the faithful will be taken up to heaven in the Rapture; seventy-four percent believe that Satan exists, whereas among Evangelicals that number increases to ninety-three percent; and seventeen percent believe the end of the world will occur in their lifetime ('The Pop Prophets', *Newsweek*, 24th May, 2004).

From the perspective of the theory of knowledge, these cases are not precisely the same. The belief in seventy-two virgins appears to be a classic example of an empirically untestable belief since, even though there may be an elaborate theological rationale for the number seventy-two, if there were seventy-one or seventy-three or none at all, no one living is ever going to know. The ritual sacrifice to obtain lottery numbers at least potentially could be subjected to empirical test to ascertain the relative frequency with which winning numbers are obtained by this method, which presumably tends toward zero as its value. And the popularity of religious beliefs does not itself imply specific actions based upon them, until you consider that those who believe include persons, such as George W. Bush, who are in powerful positions to make decisions affecting us all.

# 4.1  *Is Morality Without Religion Possible?*

It will generate little controversy to suggest that religious beliefs can be loosely classified into the broad general categories of religious beliefs about God or gods, which are theological in kind, and religious beliefs about morality, which are social or political in kind. That virtually every theological belief qualifies as an article of faith would not be widely contested. Most theologians and philosophers concede that the existence of God (in anything approximating traditional conceptions) can neither be proven nor disproven, that the existence of multiple gods—such as one for each of the seasons or for the four elements, say—can neither be proven nor disproven, and that every true believer can rest assured that, at the very least, their theological beliefs cannot be shown to be false. By the same token, they cannot be shown to be true.

According to the principle of the ethics of belief, we are morally entitled to hold a belief only if we are logically entitled to hold it. If we grant that we are logically entitled to hold beliefs about the world only when they are appropriately related by suitable inductive and deductive logical relations to available evidence on the basis of observations, measurements, and experiments, then the only conceptions of God that appear to be empirically testable are those that identify God with nature, as in the case of pantheism. We interact with the natural world in space and time, after all, unlike a transcendent world beyond space and time to which we have no access. Beliefs about God as an omniscient and omnipotent entity existing beyond space and time, therefore, are beliefs about the world that we are not entitled to hold.

That most theological beliefs about God or gods are not beliefs we are logically entitled to hold does not mean that alternative conceptions of God or gods are, on that account, beyond debate. The conception of God as the Creator suggests that it makes more sense to envision God as a woman than as a man. Women, after all, can give birth, which is something no man can do. But we are no more logically entitled to believe in God as a woman than we are to believe in God as a man. What may be even more intriguing than the status of religious beliefs about God is the status of religious beliefs about morality. The principle of the ethics of belief entails we are likewise not morally entitled to hold beliefs about morality unless we are logically entitled to hold them. This implies that many religious beliefs about morality may also be immoral unless they qualify as beliefs that we are logically entitled to hold.

Speaking generally, we are logically entitled to hold beliefs about the world only when they satisfy appropriate logical standards. We tend to assume that beliefs we can justify on the basis of direct experience are therefore justifiable, which—in the case of those who are not color-blind, tone deaf, and the like—tends to suffice in our practical lives. We can characterize this as 'ordinary knowledge'. For the purpose of this chapter and to exemplify the kinds of standards that matter here, I shall assume that a more exact conception would be codified by the most defensible account of the logical structure of scientific reasoning, which is known as *abductivism* and which incorporates inference to the best explanation, as readers of this book can discover in the Appendix. The products of this process are characterizable as 'scientific knowledge'.

When it comes to hypotheses or theories concerning the world around us, ordinary reasoning (typically implicitly) and scientific knowledge (often explicitly) proceeds through a process involving the following stages or steps:

(S1) consider the available alternatives;

(S2) consider the available relevant evidence;

(S3) reject alternatives incompatible with the available evidence;

(S4) appraise the likelihood of the alternatives in relation to the evidence to ascertain which provides the best explanation of the evidence, where the likelihood of hypothesis $h$ given evidence $e$ is equal to the probability of evidence $e$ if hypothesis $h$ were true; where

(S5) the preferable hypothesis is the one that possesses the highest likelihood in relation to the available evidence; and

(S6) the preferable hypothesis is acceptable when sufficient relevant evidence becomes available, which entails that it 'settles down'.

We typically employ these processes and procedures without reflection in our daily lives. I notice a bottle that looks like a bottle of beer in the refrigerator when I come home from work. Ordinarily, something looks like a bottle of beer because it is a bottle of beer. If I later open it and take a swig, only to discover that it tastes like fruit punch, I may have belatedly discovered that my daughter has brought home fruit punch in a bottle that looks like a beer bottle. I am thereby considering alternative hypotheses about the world around me and, perhaps less systematically than I might have preferred, discovering that there is available evidence to discount my original hypothesis in favor of an alternative as a manifestation of the tentative and fallible character of empirical knowledge and in contrast with 'articles of faith', which are often held to be absolute and infallible.

According to the ethics of belief, we are logically entitled to hold beliefs about morality only if we are logically entitled to hold them on the basis of appropriate logical standards. While it may come as some surprise, I am suggesting that the standards for evaluating alternative moral theories are comparable to those for evaluating alternative empirical theories, when properly approached. First, we must separate legality from morality and from propriety, respectively. The legal is what has the status of the law, which, in an open society, tends to be published and publicly accessible. These are behaviors punishable by the state via police, courts, and prisons. What is proper is a matter of customs, manners, and etiquette. The moral concerns how we should normally treat other persons, not necessarily by heroic self-sacrifice, which is a special case known as *supererogation*.

The moral and the legal do not necessarily coincide, since conduct can be legal even when it's immoral and can be moral even when it's illegal. Slavery offers an instructive example, since slavery is immoral if anything is immoral, yet slavery was perfectly legal for much of the history of this country. Consuming alcohol as a beverage offers another, since prior to Prohibition, it was perfectly legal, just as it became subsequently. But the moral status of consuming alcohol, unlike driving drunk or public intoxication, has remained constant and has always been, so far as I have been able to discern, perfectly moral. When disparity between the legal and the moral becomes excessive, social tensions tend to arise from the underlying inequities, which can produce unrest, passive resistance, or even civil wars. A good society maintains a suitable balance between legality and morality.

An important question thus becomes whether there are criteria of adequacy that might be employed to evaluate moral theories akin to those of inference to the best explanation for empirical theories. There appear to be three, namely:

(CA-1) an acceptable theory of morality must not reduce to the corrupt principle that *might makes right*;

(CA-2) an acceptable theory must suitably classify pre-analytically clear cases of moral and immoral behavior (where these behaviors have been virtually universally acknowledged within human societies as moral and immoral, respectively, including speaking the truth and keeping promises, on the one hand, and murder, robbery, and rape, on the other); and

(CA-3) an acceptable theory should shed light on the pre-analytically problematical cases as well, including today, for example, abortion, cloning, and stem-cell research.

Actions based upon beliefs we are not morally entitled to hold are themselves immoral unless they qualify as moral by a standard that we are logically entitled to accept. This principle harmonizes with the Roman Catholic conception of natural law, according to which we must exercise our reason to discover what God would have us do, which in turn emanates from the classic question, 'Is an action right because God wills it or does God will it because it is right?' There appears to be general agreement that the former alternative both denies the goodness of God and trivializes morality. Hence, we must exercise our reason to discover what is right in order to know what God would have us do. Here we are exercising our reason in order to know what is right, apart from any commitment to God at all.

## Eight Moral Theories Evaluated

Let's evaluate eight theories of morality, including four 'traditional' theories, which make morality a (non-rational) matter of circumstance, such as who you are or what family, religion, or culture you were born into. Employing the method of counterexample, it should be possible to establish which of these eight theories qualifies as the most defensible based upon the exercise of reason. As will become apparent, none of these theories provides a suitable foundation for the conception of morality as a set of objective and universal principles that are capable of satisfying the criteria of adequacy adopted here—with exactly one exception. This argument will draw the conclusion that it is the most defensible. (More extensive discussion may be found in Rachels 1999 and Rachels 2003.)

According to the first theory (T1), *subjectivism*, an action A is right (for person P) if P approves of A. This theory, which exerts appeal on freshmen students, implies that morality can vary from person to person and from time to time depending on each person's attitudes and values. If a person were malevolent and wanted to bring about your murder, rape, or robbery, then if this theory were correct, it would be mistaken to suggest that his action in doing that was immoral. On the contrary, if that person approved of that action, then, no matter how much you might deplore it, that action would be morally right—for him. The same obtains for everyone else, which means that this theory not only qualifies as pre-analytically immoral behavior as moral but also reduces to the corrupt principle that might makes right. (T1) therefore violates (CA-1) and (CA-2) and should be rejected.

According to the second theory, (T2), *family values*, an action A is right (for family F) if F approves of A. This approach effects a generalization of (T1) by substituting the attitudes and values of the family for those of the individual. But its consequences are no more defensible. Consider, for example, the Archie Bunker family, the Charles Manson family, or the family featured in *The Texas Chain Saw Massacre*. While Archie was merely a bigot who was anti-Jew, anti-black, and anti-gay, Charlie actually attempted to start a war between blacks and whites by sending his followers to commit murders to trigger it off. And it does not take gruesome chainsaw killings to appreciate that (T2), like (T1) before it, similarly violates (CA-1) and (CA-2) and, on that basis, must likewise be rejected.

According to the third theory, (T3), *religious ethics*, an action A is right (for religion R) if R approves of A. The problems are no doubt already apparent from consideration of (T1) and (T2). There are many religions, including polytheism, monotheism, pantheism, deism, Buddhism, Confucianism, Taoism, Brahmanism, Hinduism, Zoroastrianism, Mohammedanism (Islam), Judaism, Christianity (Roman Catholicism, Protestantism, Fundamentalism, Assembly of God, . . . ), which adhere to different articles of faith. While most would agree that actions such as murder, rape, and robbery are wrong, they tend to disagree on precisely why. And if you don't find one that you like, you are entitled to found a religion of your own, even if you happen to be the only member! So religious ethics does not look promising.

Fundamentalists, who maintain that the Bible is the literal word of God, could take exception on the grounds a religious text, 'the Word of God', is authoritative, not any particular religious tradition. But taking the Bible literally in relation to moral maxims produces problems, insofar as moral maxims to be found in religious texts, such as the Bible, are not always plausible candidates for moral truths. According to the Book of Leviticus, Chapter 20: Verse 9, for example, "If anyone curses his father or mother, he must be [not grounded; not given time out; not sent to his room; but] put to death." Or consider Verse 10: "If a man commits adultery with another man's wife—with the wife of his neighbor—both the adulterer and the adulteress must be put to death." While this might do wonders to relieve overcrowding in Southern California, I doubt many of us regard it as a good idea.

There are many more. According to Verse 27, for example: "A man or a woman who is a medium or spiritualist among you must be put to death. You are to stone them; their blood will be on their own heads." There goes Dionne Warwick and the Psychic Network! Or, for the sake of variation, consider Deuteronomy, Chapter 25: Verses 11–12: "If two men are fighting and the wife of one of them comes to rescue her husband from his assailant, and she reached out and grabs him by his private parts, you shall cut off her hand. Show her no pity." Personally, if some big bruiser were pounding me, I would be grateful to my wife for her assistance in getting him off me. I would want to shake her hand, not cut it off! And the problems with citing religious leaders, I presume, are equally apparent, whether we have in mind Jerry Falwell, Pat Robertson, Jim Jones, or Jimmy Swaggart. We cannot know which among them exemplifies moral virtue without already knowing which traits are moral traits.

The fourth theory, (T4), *cultural relativism*, according to which an action A is right (in culture C) if C approves of A, suffers from similar shortcomings. Can cultures in which polygamy, polyandry, cannibalism, or female genital mutilation are practiced all be equally right and equally moral? If this approach were correct, the answer would be, 'Yes!' I have argued that virtually universal human experience qualifies murder, robbery, and rape, for example, as immoral within the society or group, a finding that is supported by studying different cultures. But it succumbs to (CA-1), nevertheless, since vast numbers of human beings have been deliberately killed in the name of religions and of cultures. Serbs and Muslims, Arabs and Jews, Sunnis, Shiites and Kurds exemplify a few of the variations in play around the world today, and there are many more. They may not succeed and they may not prevail, but as long as these actions conform to a cultural standards, they cannot be morally wrong.

The traditional theories suffer from a common defect, namely: they make moral criticism, moral progress, and moral reform meaningless conceptions. If a person (a family, a religion, or a culture) changes its attitudes about the kinds of actions that it approves and disapproves, such as by abandoning female genital mutilation, say, in African tribes, that cannot represent moral progress, but merely a change in the prevailing attitude. No matter what attitude prevails at a time, so long as it is the prevailing attitude, actions in conformity with it are right and deviations are wrong. Problems with traditional theories motivate consideration of different principles that might function as a theoretical foundation for moral theory, where I shall consider four. While they are more defensible than their traditional counterparts, only one of them appears to be capable of satisfying criteria of adequacy (CA-1) to (CA-3).

Three of them are consequentialist accounts, according to which an action A is right when it produces at least as much of The Good as any available alternative. Historically, candidates for The Good (which is supposed to be valuable in and of itself) have included happiness, pleasure, knowledge, power, and (least plausibly) money. Although there may be latitude for debate, I shall assume that the most defensible conception of The Good is happiness. The issue that then arises is this: whose happiness should matter? And the answer to that question generates the difference between three species of consequentialism, the first of which is known as 'ethical egoism'. According to our fifth theory, (T5), *ethical egoism*, an action A is right when it produces at least as much happiness for person P as any available alternative. Plug in Ted Bundy, John Gacy, or Jeffrey Dahmer as the value of 'P', however, and it should be apparent that (T5) violates both (CA-1) and (CA-2).

After all, if someone derives more happiness from murder, robbery, or rape than from any available alternative, then those actions are morally right if (T5) were correct. And as long as that person is able to impose his will upon others, his actions do not qualify as morally wrong. The situation is not salvaged by the generalization of consequentialism to groups, moreover, where our sixth theory, (T6) *limited utilitarianism*, maintains that an action A is right when it produces at least as much happiness for group G as any alternative. Let the value of 'G' range over the Third Reich, the Mafia, or even General Motors, however, and it should be obvious that, even if territorial expansion, military aggression, and systematic genocide produce more happiness for Nazis than any alternative, it does not make those practices moral. (T6) clearly violates (CA-1) and (CA-2).

Because groups can be far more efficient, effective, and reliable in bringing about its aims, objectives, and goals, limited utilitarianism turns out to be the most pernicious of moral theories. The most important problem with both of these varieties appears to be that, in making moral judgments, they exclude from consideration consequences for anyone other than the person himself (in the case of ethical egoism) or than members of the group (in the case of limited utilitarianism). Consequences for others, no matter how dire, do not count! It follows that no actions whatever, including assassination, mutilation or genocide, are inherently morally wrong, because no actions are inherently morally wrong. If taking such actions would produce more happiness for the person or for the group, those actions would be right actions, were either of these theories correct.

The seventh theory, (T7), *classic utilitarianism*, therefore, appears to be more defensible, insofar as it maintains that an action A is right when it produces at least as much happiness for everyone as any alternative. This is the first theory that requires that the consequences of actions for everyone who is affected by them has to be taken into account in determining the morality of those actions. Since some persons may be made happier and others less happy by decisions that affect them, classic utilitarianism trades, not in happiness per se, but net happiness as gross happiness minus gross unhappiness. So an action is right, on this account, when it produces more net happiness than any other option.

Classic utilitarianism represents a giant step in the right direction because it requires taking into account the consequences for everyone affected by an action and not merely those for the person or the group performing it. But it harbors covert problems. Suppose, for example, that a social arrangement in which eighty-five percent of the population were masters and fifteen percent were slaves was the one that produced the greatest net happiness? Suppose that, although the slaves would be far less happy, the masters would be so much happier that this exact distribution produced more net happiness than any alternative arrangement? Would that make it moral? Since slavery is immoral, if any action is immoral, it should be apparent that the very prospect of justifying a slave-based society on classic utilitarian grounds demonstrates that something is profoundly wrong.

Even through the formula, 'The greatest good for the greatest number', has been enshrined as though it reflected a basic axiom of moral theory, it cannot be sustained. The greatest good for the greatest number as the maximization of net happiness could be used to justify a slave-based society! The problem, moreover, is not unique to this example. Suppose that the government were to round up one hundred smokers at random each year, put them on television and shoot them. What might be the expected effects? Probably enthusiasm for smoking would diminish; there would be fewer incidents of lung cancer, cardiovascular disease, and such; the cost of health insurance would drop; people would live longer, healthier lives. It might even produce more net happiness than any available option. So should we be rounding up smokers and shooting them?

## 4.2  *Abortion, Stem-Cells, and Cloning.*

As students of political science are well aware, the principle of majority rule must be supplemented by principles of minority rights, lest the noble concept of democratic rule degenerate into no more than the tyranny of the mob.

A more defensible approach toward understanding morality, (T8), is *a deontological theory*, according to which an action A is right when it involves treating other persons as ends and never merely as means. Treating others 'as ends' means treating them as valuable in and of themselves, which may be encapsulated in the notion of always treating other persons with respect. Persons are thus entities with interests that are entitled to due consideration. If this is the most defensible conception of morality, as I shall contend, then it also demonstrates that some religious maxims, such as 'the Golden Rule' of doing unto others as you would have them do unto you, are correct, not because they are religious maxims but because they are logically justifiable.

(T8) does not mean that persons should never treat others as means but that persons should never treat others *merely* as means. We all treat one another as means all the time. Employers treat their employees as means to run a business and make a profit, while employees treat their employers as means to earn an income and make a living. As long as they are not treating each other with disrespect—by employers, for example, offering substandard wages, excess hours of employment, or unsafe work conditions; by employees clocking in for work not performed, stealing from their employer, or failing to perform the tasks for which they were hired—these can be moral relationships. Similarly for doctors and patients, lawyers and clients, students and teachers.

There are other accounts of morality, including the *social contract* theory. Sometimes characterized as 'morality by agreement', there appears to be no reason why a community might not agree to a slave-based society, betting that they would be among the eighty-five percent who are masters! That would be 'immorality by agreement'. Sociobiologists have advanced selfish genes, kin selection, reciprocal altruism, and social cooperation as the biological foundation of morality. They can be readily refuted on the basis of counterexamples, however, where selfish genes justify serial rape; kin selection, hiring an unqualified cousin over a qualified non-relative; reciprocal altruism, engaging in insider-trading; and social co-operation, military agression, territorial conquest, and systematic genocide (Fetzer 2005). It becomes increasingly clear that morality does not invariably advance our genetic self-interest, which means that, properly understood, morality transcends biology.

Only deontological theory appears capable of satisfying (CA-1) and (CA-2), while explaining why practices that are virtually universally condemned, such as murder, robbery, and rape, are immoral practices, and why practices that are virtually universally endorsed, such as keeping promises and speaking the truth, are moral practices. The former involve treating other persons merely as means, while the latter involve treating other persons with respect. There are situations, however, in which speaking the truth or promise keeping might conflict with morality. A spy caught behind enemy lines, for example, should not reveal the network of agents with whom she has been working because it would be wrong not to speak the truth. There are circumstances in which the right thing to do would be to remain silent or to deliberately misinform others.

Practices such as speaking the truth and keeping promises have exceptions, which makes them 'rules of thumb' that are usually correct but sometimes not. Consideration must be given to the totality of circumstances in determining the right thing to do. Actions are right when they involve treating other persons with respect, which is a consequence of treating them as ends and not merely as means. But the consequences for you personally with respect to happiness do not matter. That's why a poor man who returns a wallet is doing the right thing, even if it does not enhance his happiness. A spy might therefore lie to save the lives of the network of agents with whom she has worked without violating deontological standards, especially in an adversarial context where speaking the truth would betray them. That would be the right thing to do.

Persons as persons have moral rights and incur obligations to treat others with respect, but not when others are violating those rights and not fulfilling their own obligations. Hence, there is no moral obligation to cooperate with those who violate morality. Interestingly, however, there might nevertheless be legal obligations to cooperate with those who violate morality, as with the whistleblower who abrogates contractual obligations to his company in order to expose crime and corruption. These are *bona fide* acts of supererogation, which all too often led to the punishment of those who sacrifice themselves for the sake of the common good, a conception that, in this time in history, almost appears quaint. But it reflects one more example of the possibility that the moral and the legal need not coincide, which is of primary concern.

So there can be conflicts between rules of thumb and exceptions to those rules. Even murder might be justifiable under special conditions. Some writers have speculated that, if attempts to assassinate Adolf Hitler or Josef Stalin had been successful, many lives might have been spared. Since murder involves the deliberate killing of a person that is illegal, however, there is clearly room for debate over whether killing Hitler or Stalin would have been wrong. A tyrant who massively violates deontological principles by treating others with severe disrespect deserves to be punished, where the extent, duration, and intensity of their crimes may dictate extreme measures. Yet there's a virtually universal consensus on the fundamental importance of due process for those accused of crimes, prisoners of war, and even unlawful combatants.

The contrast case, of course, is that of taking the life, not of a tyrant, such as Hitler or Stalin, but of an innocent, as in the case of abortion. The capacity to deal with cases like abortion, stem-cell research, and cloning is a crucial test of a theory relative to pre-analytically problematical cases. The slogan, 'Abortion is murder', raises the crucial questions of whether (a) the developing entity properly qualifies as a person and (b) whether killing the developing entity properly qualifies as wrongful. Since abortions are legal under *Roe v. Wade* (1973), question (b) is not whether killing the developing entity is legally wrong, which it is not, but whether it is morally wrong. It's morally wrong if it involves treating a person without respect and merely as a means. This in turn implies that the crucial question about abortion is whether the entity under consideration properly qualifies as a person. So the key question is (a).

Gestation for human beings tends to be divided into stages by weeks, where the fertilized ovum (zygotic) stage is the first two weeks after conception, the early developmental (embryonic) stage is from the second to the eighth week after conception, while the mid to late developmental (fetal) stage is from the ninth through the thirty-eighth week of gestation, following which (for a normal pregnancy) a live birth occurs. If we accept (T8) as the most defensible theory of morality and explore its ramifications for abortion and stem-cell research, it follows that abortion and stem-cell research are immoral only if they involve treating other persons without due respect. The question is not whether these are stages in the development of a human being or whether or not life begins at conception. Those are questions whose answers are obvious and affirmative.

Do zygotes, embryos, and fetuses qualify as persons in the sense of social and moral entities that can have interests and that have to be treated with respect? Are they persons as entities with interests that are entitled to due consideration? Given the ethics of belief, this question cannot be properly answered based on articles of faith. Even if the Roman Catholic Church, for example, maintains the doctrine of ensoulment— that the soul enters the body at conception—this does not qualify as an acceptable solution to the problem. The presence or absence of souls is not accessible, directly or indirectly, to observation, measurement, or experiment, and cannot satisfy the condition of logical entitlement on the basis of inductive or deductive reasoning. Three possible sources of information that might matter in answering this question, however, include ordinary language, embryology, and law, especially the Supreme Court's decision in *Roe v. Wade*.

No unambiguous answer to this question appears to be derivable from the use of ordinary language. According to *Webster's New World Dictionary*, Third College Edition (1988), the term has a variety of senses, such as the following:

> **person** = df 1. a human being, especially as distinguished from a thing or lower animal; individual man, woman, or child. . . . 3. a) a living human body b) bodily form or appearance (to be neat about one's person) 4. personality; self; being; . . . 7. Law any individual or incorporated group having certain legal rights and responsibilities 8. Christian theol. any of the three modes of being (Father, Son, and Holy Ghost) in the Trinity.

The notion of 'a living human body' suggests that to be a person an entity must have a separate existence, which hints that even fetuses may not qualify under ordinary language criteria. Certainly, the notion of 'personality' appears to be highly inappropriate for zygotes and embryos, especially, though some women report behavior by their fetuses during later stages indicative of personalities. At best, the use of the word 'person' in ordinary language appears to suggest that zygotes and embryos are only early stages in the development of persons.

Nor can the problem be resolved by appealing to medical embryology. The stages of embryonic development, for example, proceed through the fertilized ovum to blastocysts and villus formation on to entities that resemble shrimp or seahorses far more than they do human beings. Were morphological similarity the standard for personhood, then there would be no basis for making such a claim prior to the seventh week or later (Sadler 1990). Consider, for example, the appearance of the developing entity at day 36, day 37, day 38, and day 39:

**Figure 4.1** Some Stages in Embryogenesis

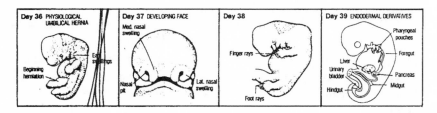

At best, morphological similarities to live births likewise suggests that zygotes and embryos are no more than early stages in the development of persons. And surely that is what we should expect, since embryology is not a source of social and moral concepts but rather the study of the various stages of human gestation.

The prospect that zygotes and embryos are no more than early stages in the development of persons becomes important within the framework of the ethics of belief, because if they do not qualify as 'persons', then the they are not kinds of entities that are capable of having interests that require due consideration. In that case, abortions are not murder, because they do not involve the deliberate killing of a person that is morally wrong. Indeed, this turns out to be the case on two grounds, since (a) they are not persons at all and (b) they are not among the kinds of entities that it would be morally wrong to kill. (Even the deliberate killing of persons is not always considered to be morally wrong, as the examples of soldiers in combat, police in the performance of their duties, and civilians in self-defense display.) The non-person alternative would seem to be to consider the developing entity as a special kind of property, which may appropriately be entitled to special forms of protection under the law.

The Supreme Court in *Roe v. Wade* (1973) considered several criteria for the performance of abortions and divided the cycle of gestation into trimesters (three three-month long intervals). The Court decided that the government had no compelling rationale for interfering with abortions during the first three months of gestation, when they are unrestrictedly permissible, but that it had an interest in protecting women in relation to abortions during the second three months of gestation, when how they were to be conducted could be subject to regulation. In relation to the third trimester, the Court held that abortions were permissible but only to preserve the life or the health of the woman. Conservatives have bridled at this ruling, claiming that abortions should be permissible only in the case of rape, incest, or to save the life of the mother and for no other reason. Some very few oppose it even in these cases.

Perhaps the most interesting aspect of the Court's ruling was the division of the cycle of pregnancy into trimesters, which can be correlated, at least approximately, with the development of the fetus, such that heart function has been established and brain activity is detectable by the end of the first trimester; brain function has been established and viability attained by the end of the second trimester; and a live birth typically occurs at the end of the third trimester, as the following diagram displays:

**Figure 4.2** The Court's Trimester Division

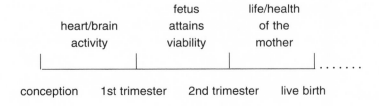

Thus, although the Court preserved the concept of personhood for the issue of live births, it could be argued that it was imposing a graduated scale of personhood for which the earliest stage occurs at the end of the second trimester, where the entity first deserves to be treated as of a kind capable of having interests that require due consideration; at this stage only, there are considerations in favor of a 'right to life' of the fetus, provided it does not conflict with a woman's right to preserve her health and her life, should a tension develop between them.

The strongest inference that could be drawn from *Roe v. Wade* is that a person is a human fetus that has attained the status of viability. And that, indeed, appears to be a responsible position to adopt. It represents a vastly better reasoned approach than to assume that zygotes and embryos are persons. Legal rights and responsibilities, after all, are distributed attendant upon attaining certain standing in the community, often as a function of a person's age. In most states, a person can obtain a driver's license at age fifteen, can marry without their parents' consent at age eighteen, and can vote in political elections at age twenty-one. Their governments assume corresponding duties and obligations to protect those rights. This graduated theory of rights and responsibilities is pervasive in human societies.

No one would argue that infants or children should be able to drive, to marry, or to vote, which supports the conception of graduated rights that are contingent upon reaching certain stages of development, where the 'right to life' of a fetus is only the first in a series of rights that increase with stages of development. And what if zygotes and embryos were persons? Governments would at the very least possess obligations to ensure their 'right to life' by such intrusive measures as, for example, mandatory monthly pregnancy testing; tracking the distribution of semen; monitoring sexual intercourse; promoting the 'adoption' of unwanted zygotes and embryos; and otherwise enforcing their legal rights. The situation would be absurd.

This does not mean that the Supreme Court has had the last word, even though in a case of this kind it must have the final say. It could be argued that advances in technology make 'viability' a shifting criterion. Today, in a well-equipped neonatal intensive care unit, survival in an artificial womb can sometimes be achieved at twenty-two weeks. But there are at least two responses to this observation, the first of which is that viability means survivability independently of any womb, natural or artificial. I happen to believe that is a defensible position to maintain. But if it were not, the Court might still have reached the right decision on the basis of the wrong premise.

Once we have cleared away the religious beliefs that tend to obfuscate the relevant issues, it becomes apparent that the normative notion of personhood as a social, legal, or moral concept needs to be suitably correlated with descriptive personhood as a scientific, empirical, or testable property. We need a criterion, such as viability, as a generally reliable but not therefore infallible standard. The deontological theory of morality, moreover, at the minimum implies the harm principle—namely, that it is morally wrong to inflict physical harm upon persons in the absence of their consent—which typically implies the presence of sentience or consciousness (ordinarily, the existence of the capacity to experience pain). Sentience would therefore appear to provide an alternative to viability as a preferable conception of the earliest stages of personhood.

A suitable normative conception could define 'persons' as genetic humans at or beyond the stage of sentience or consciousness and capable of suffering pain. In the absence of sentience or consciousness, the developing entities are not persons. In that case, prior to sentience, abortions do not involve the killing of persons and are not necessarily morally wrong. The corresponding descriptive property becomes cerebral cortical and CNS development at or beyond the stage sufficient for sentience or consciousness, which appears to coincide with the Court's end of the second trimester on different grounds (Kandel 2000; Bear 2001). On either the viability criterion or the sentience criterion, therefore, the Supreme Court's decision appears to be defensible, even though a host of issues remain about the nature of consciousness and mentality.

An intriguing counterexample to this approach, however, arises from the fact that some persons are born without the capacity for the sensation of pain (Bear 2001, p. 422). Even by describing them as 'persons', I agree it would be wrong to deny that they are persons as genetic human beings who are the products of live births but who lack the nociceptive system that warns most of us of the danger of damage to ourselves relative to painful stimuli. These persons therefore run risks and tend to live shorter lives than normal persons equipped with the ability to feel pain. This suggests that, as in the case of viabililty, the standard should be understood as the stage at which pain sensitivity is ordinarily present during fetal development. As a criterion of personhood, however, sentience can serve as a generally reliable but not therefore infallible rule of thumb, where viability would still be considered to be the more viable alternative definition.

# 4.3  *Consciousness and Personhood*

The conception of graduated rights that accrue at different stages in the life of a person supports the inference that, prior to viability, an entity that could develop into a human being has no 'right to life', especially in a conflict with those of the woman who bears it. Sentience, however, understood as implying the capacity to experience pain, serves as a (possibly more defensible) alternative to viability for justifying the proportional attribution of conditional personhood to the developing fetus, where the fetus having attained the stage of sentience has a 'right to life' as long as it does not conflict with or adversely affect the life or the health of its bearer. On either viability or sentience criteria, there seems to be an appropriate correlation between the normative conception of personhood and its descriptive counterpart.

A theory of graduated rights parallels similar proportionment of value in other domains. The acorn that has the potential to become a mighty oak, for example, is not valued as greatly as the mighty oak. Indeed, there is a continuum of increasing value as the acorn turns into a sprig and then a small tree and eventually grows to become a useful form of timber. (The reason why the Bush Administration's claim that there are more trees now than there were twenty years ago is misleading is that those that exist today are younger and less valuable than those that have been cropped.) Apart from the context of abortion, there are many examples of graduated values, such as the new hire as opposed to the trainee as opposed to the experienced worker. None of us would be inclined to think twice about experienced workers being paid more for their work than new hires. A new hire may have the potential to become a trained employee, but no one would suppose that he should be paid the same on that ground.

The investigation of these questions could be carried further by considering the prospect that consciousness might matter here. The most defensible conception of consciousness derives from the theory of minds as sign-using (or 'semiotic') systems, where signs are things that stand for other things. On this approach, minds turn out to be properties of brains or, at least, of various kinds of systems of neurons, which can be extremely primitive (Fetzer 2002; 2005). There are three basic kinds of signs: iconic (things that resemble that for which they stand), indexical (things that are causes or effects of that for which they stand), and symbolic (things that are merely habitually associated with that for which they stand). Species tend to differ relative to the kinds of signs they can use and the range of signs within the kinds they utilize.

Thus, photos, statues, and paintings (at least when they are realistic or naturalistic in kind) are iconic in resembling what they stand for. Anything can resemble other things in some respects without resembling them in every respect. My driver's license photo, for example, resembles me when viewed straight on (on not such a great day, perhaps), but not when it is turned on its side (because I am just not that thin)! Fire, smoke, and ashes all stand for one another as causes or effects of each other. Symptoms of diseases are other examples of indices, where it may take an expert to diagnose them (read the signs). Words and sentences are among the most familiar example of symbols, where ordinary languages represent systems of habitual associations between (written or spoken) words and things.

A red light at an intersection can function as an icon insofar as it resembles the color of the dress your wife wore the evening before. It functions as an index for a transportation department worker who has been sent out to repair it because it is stuck on red and won't change. And it functions as a symbol for those who are know the rules of the road, for whom it stands for applying the breaks and coming to a complete halt and only proceeding when the light changes to green. The fact that a husband whose wife has gone into labor and wants to get to the hospital as soon as possible, who consequently cautiously runs the light when he has checked for cross traffic, does not alter the meaning of that sign. He knows its meaning, but his motives and ethics override it. He has more urgent responsibilities than to conform to traffic regulations when his wife's water has broken. So he runs the light instead.

Pursuing this approach, consciousness is relative to signs of specific kinds: a system is conscious (with respect to signs of kind S) when it has the ability to use signs of kind S and is not incapacitated from the exercise of that ability. Similarly, cognition is an effect that occurs as the outcome of a causal interaction between a system that is conscious with respect to signs of kind S and the presence of a sign of kind S within suitable causal proximity. It does not require rocket science to recognize that fetuses, even in the third trimester, have extremely limited capacity for the use of signs. Consciousness for them turns out to be extremely primitive, and occurrences of cognition must be extremely few and far between. That is not to say it does not occur at all, but rather that the use of signs by a fetus—where signs, unlike mere stimuli, painful or not, are meaningful by virtue of standing for something for the sign user—is virtually nil. So appeals to consciousness and cognition do not support the case for fetal personhood.

This result implies that the mental capacities of the fetus, even in the later stages of pregnancy, are extremely limited. The difference between stimuli that function as causes of responses in the fetus, such as painful stimuli that may induce avoidance response, and stimuli that serve as signs that are meaningful for the fetus by virtue of standing for something for that fetus deserves to be emphasized. The possession of a neurological system—a brain—is not identical to the capacity to exercise the use of signs—a mind. This suggests a potentially even more powerful criterion for personhood that might eventually become more important in deliberations over issues of this kind. The possession of sentience and viability are not the same thing as the possession of mentality or semiotic ability, which, presupposes a point of view. Since semiotic abilities appear to be extremely limited, if not non-existent, during pregnancy, the adoption of the capacity to use signs as a criterion of personhood strongly reinforces the exclusion of early-term fetuses.

Some women have maintained that their fetuses, during later stages of pregnancy, became accustomed to their voice and tended to respond to it. Anecdotal evidence, of course, is vastly weaker than controlled experiments, but in the interest of covering all the bases, suppose we assume that that is true, namely: that at least some fetuses in the late stages of pregnancy display behavior within the womb that their mothers interpret as responding to the sound of their voices. In that case, it could be argued that, for those fetuses, the sound of their voices is functioning as a sign—presumably, of love and affection—for them as sign users, in which case the semiotic criterion would support the case for personhood, after all. Such phenomena, assuming they take place, however, would selectively support the standing of late-term or third-trimester fetuses as possessing the status of persons with a qualified right to life, which I have accepted on other grounds.

Many examples illustrate that the use of signs presupposes a point of view. Since my driver's license photo may resemble my facial appearance viewed from the front but not from the side, discerning the resemblance relation depends upon adopting the right point of view. Nothing could exemplify that more clearly than the case of the red light at an intersection. Taken as an icon, it resembles the color of a dress. Taken as an index, it displays the effects of malfunction. Taken as a symbol, it induces most drivers, under ordinary conditions, to adapt their behavior to its instructions.

None of these 'stand for' relations is inherent in a sign-user absent a point of view. And this, in turn, suggests another potential criterion of personhood, which is *having a point of view*. While there could be a convergence of opinion about what kinds of treatment, for example, might or not be in the interests of a fetus, it is difficult to imagine any justification for claiming a fetus has a point of view, which affords another foundation for denying that fetuses should qualify as persons. But, as before, it may be said that late-term fetuses are developing in that direction.

The principal conclusions of this investigation are therefore as follows:

(C1)  We are not logically entitled to hold the belief that stem cells, zygotes, embryos, or early-term fetuses are 'persons' on the basis of theological religious beliefs.

(C2)  We are not logically entitled to hold the belief that abortion and stem cell research are immoral on the basis of theological religious beliefs.

(C3)  We are not logically entitled to hold the belief that abortion and stem-cell research are immoral on the basis of social or political religious beliefs unless they can be shown to be immoral on the basis of deontological standards.

(C4)  In order to be shown to be immoral on the basis of deontological standards, it would be necessary to show that stem cells, zygotes, embryos, and early-term fetuses properly qualify as 'persons' in the moral sense.

(C5)  Neither ordinary language nor medical embryology nor the Supreme Court provide any logical entitlement to conclude that stem cells, zygotes, embryos or early-term fetuses properly qualify as 'persons' in the appropriate sense.

(C6)  Appeals to sentience and to viability appear to provide objective criteria supporting the view that late-term fetuses may properly qualify as 'persons' in the absence of stronger standards.

(C7)  Consciousness and cognition as characteristics of the possession of mentality appear to provide a stronger standard, but it is one which supports and reinforces distinctions between early stage and late-term fetuses.

(C8)  Moreover, there seems to be no other non-theological basis for qualifying early stage fetuses as 'persons'.

(C9)  It follows that we are not logically justified in holding the belief that early term fetuses properly qualify as 'persons'.

(C10) Since we are not logically entitled to hold that belief, therefore, we are also not morally entitled to hold it.

It follows that the slogan, 'Abortion is murder', cannot be sustained for taking the life of early-term fetuses, since they do not properly qualify as persons. Yet even though women may voluntarily choose abortions, that does not give anyone else the right to bring about the termination of their pregnancies. It's quite consistent to view killing a pregnant woman as worse than killing a non-pregnant woman, just as we view it as worse to kill someone and burn down their house than simply to kill them. One reasonable approach would be to treat fetuses as a type of private property, one so special that it merits explicit recognition under the law.

Since the treatment of early-term fetuses as persons cannot be logically justified and thereby violates the ethics of belief, even religious persons who interfere with the right of others to abortions and stem-cell research—no matter how sincere their beliefs or moral their lives in other respects—are pursuing unethical policies.

This extends to the debate over cloning, which has even reached into the United Nations ('UN to Consider Whether to Ban Some, or All, Forms of Cloning of Human Embryos', *New York Times*, 3rd November, 2003). The primary focus has been on reproductive cloning, which produces an offspring that is genetically identical with its parent, rather than on therapeutic cloning, which can be used to produce tissues and organs for replacement or transplantation. Opposition here, as in the case of abortion and stem-cell research, is largely rooted in the religious doctrine that even the earliest stages of gestation are entities that deserve legal protection. When these arguments are excluded from policy debates, the issues can be addressed with less emotion and greater clarify. The use of reproductive cloning for infertile couples, who would like to have offspring as closely related to them as possible, appears to be a perfectly moral and appropriate procedure.

The conclusion that abortion, stem-cell research, and cloning appear to be perfectly moral and appropriate procedures when properly understood from the perspective of the ethics of belief does not mean that they are applicable without restriction. Even when we are not dealing with persons and they are morally permissible, special conditions may still apply. The use of stem cells for research—no matter whether embryonic, umbilical, or adult—should only be pursued with the consent of the donor. Abortions—no matter whether first, second, or third trimester—should only occur as voluntary actions with the consent of the woman. During the second trimester, they can still be regulated by the state and, during the third trimester, should only be performed to preserve the health or to save the life of the mother. And exploitative cloning for immoral purposes, such as to produce slaves, should obviously be impermissible. Clones post-second trimester, are just as much persons as anyone else. A summary of the situation is as follows:

**Table 4.1**  A Summary Overview

|  | Persons? | Morally Permissible? | Special Conditions? |
|---|---|---|---|
| Embryonic Stem Cells | NO | YES | Consent |
| Umbilical Cord Stem Cells | NO | YES | Consent |
| Adult Stem Cells | NO | YES | Consent |
| Abortions (1st trimester) | NO | YES | Choice |
| Abortions (2nd trimester) | NO | YES | Regulated |
| Abortions (3rd trimester) | YES | NO | Only to save the mother's life or health |
| Therapeutic Cloning (pre-third trimester) | NO | YES | Regulated |
| Reproductive Cloning (post-second trimester) | YES | YES | For infertile couples |
| Exploitative Cloning (post-second trimester) | YES | NO | NO |

The politicization of religion which prevails in the Bush Administration, together with advances in technology, has put issues of this kind front and center in the political arena. The government restricts research that has the greatest potential to deal with some of the most debilitating of human problems, such as Alzheimer's and Parkinson's, diabetes, and other inherited diseases.

Opposition based on the belief that life begins at conception is not only misconceived—since the issue is the onset of personhood and not whether life begins at conception—but, given the ethics of belief, is not even moral. If we are to regain control of scientific research and its enormous potential to enhance the quality of life, then we must restrict the influence of religious beliefs on public policy debates. There are some promising signs, happily, as universities seek private funding to pursue stem-cell research ('U of M Plans Embryo Research', *Duluth News Tribune*, 9th February, 2004; '2 New Efforts to Develop Stem Cell Line for Study', *New York Times*, 7th June, 2006); 'U.S. Scientists Seek to Clone Human Embryos', *Duluth News Tribune*, 7th June 2006.

Indeed, the stem-cell debate verges on the absurd, insofar as most of the embryos used for harvesting their cells would otherwise be discarded. Does the Christian Right seriously believe that it makes more sense— from either a logical or a moral point of view—to simply discard these cells rather than use them for the potential benefit of human beings? This appears to be one more example where ideology over-rides sensibility and irrational beliefs improperly affect public policy.

The right to life of a late-term fetus, however, is not absolute but relative to the rights of its mother. When those rights conflict, those of the mother—as an adult whose rights outweigh those of a fetus—are properly given precedence. Hence, a late-term fetus has a right to life that can be overridden by risks to the health and life of its parent. Women who want to control their bodies, which is a very basic right, would be well advised to avoid sex with men who do not respect them. Before a woman engages in sex with a man, she should gain his acknowledgment that she has the right to decide what should be done in the case of an unplanned pregnancy. In the absence of that assurance, the best policy would appear to be, 'Just say, "No!"'

The conclusions that I have drawn could be contested on various grounds, including, for example, that there are other moral theories that need consideration, such as virtue theory. None of them appears to be as defensible as deontological theory, however, an approach that exerts profound influence in the world today through documents such as the Declaration of Independence, The Constitution of the United States, and The UN Declaration of Human Rights, all of which are based upon deontology. Utilitarianism can still serve as an appropriate foundation for decision-making in a democracy but cannot function properly without being rooted in human rights.

The Ethics of Belief imposes a very high standard. Most persons may find that standard psychologically impossible to satisfy in their personal lives, where they find belief in God or in heaven and hell irresistible. But that does not entail the right to impose those beliefs upon others who may not share them. Democracy degenerates into mob rule when majority votes can overpower the rights of minorities.

The integrity of the United States as a democratic republic founded upon the separation of church and state requires a vigorous defense. Immoral policies should be excluded from public policy debates. Religious persons who interfere with abortions, stem-cell research, and cloning—no matter how sincere their beliefs or moral their lives in other respects—are practicing immoral politics. It must come to an end. Democracy requires no less.

CHAPTER 5

# Religion, Morality, and the New American Fascism

➻ *There is a moral case for the legality of activities like flag-burning, prostitution, and pot-smoking*

➻ *Corporations become immoral when they subordinate everything to the pursuit of profit*

➻ *America is becoming fascist because the government is controlled by morally irresponsible corporations*

➻ *The Bush administration is crushing liberties at home while wreaking mayhem abroad in contravention of international law*

➻ *American policy represents the triumph of the most corrupt form of morality: the pursuit of the interests of one's own exclusive group*

*A*rticles of faith and scientific hypotheses are profoundly different. Articles of faith are unconditional, untestable, and held to be true without risking refutation. Scientific hypotheses are conditional, are testable, and will always be relinquished under suitable conditions.

In science, different investigators relying upon the same evidence, the same alternatives, and the same rules of inquiry would tend to accept, reject, and hold in suspense the same hypotheses. No such standards prevail within the domain of religious dogma. There is no counterpart to the principle of inference to the best explanation that brings about a convergence in the inferences drawn based upon the same body of evidence and alternative hypotheses.

Anyone can believe that God is male or that God is female and no one can prove that they are wrong. Unfortunately, that means no one can prove that God is not a woman any more than any one can prove that God is a man! Those who want to rely upon reason in forming their beliefs should consider agnosticism, which acknowledges that neither the existence nor the non-existence of God can be demonstrated.

This is not to deny that one or the other of those propositions must be true. As Aristotle observed, for every proposition, $p$, which makes an assertion, either $p$ is true or it is not the case that $p$ is true. There's no third alternative, which is why this principle is known as *the law of excluded middle*. Aristotle also identified the law of non-contradiction, which holds that, for every proposition $p$, it is not the case that $p$ is both true and false. They jointly imply that every proposition $p$ is either true or false, but not both.

So given a definition of 'God', it will be the case that, under each such definition, either God exists or it is not the case that God exists. But it does not follow that we could ever know which is which. That depends, in part, upon the precise meaning ascribed to the word 'God'. If 'God' is an old man who lives on a mountain, presumably we could travel to that location and search for him. If we found him, we would know that God exists under that definition. If 'God' is an omniscient, omnipotent, and omnibenevolent entity, whose existence transcends space and time, however, then matters are not so straightforward.

With regard to such a God, the problem of evil raises doubts in many minds, which ministers, priests, and rabbis often attempt to assuage. The enduring distress of the human species, however, with respect to terrorism, AIDS, and pandemics, has the capacity to raise questions even for those who are inclined to believe but who would like to know that their beliefs are rationally well-founded, or if not that, are at least not wildly indefensible. The most rational attitude toward the existence of God in his classic manifestations is agnosticism. Since the non-existence of God can no more be proven than can the existence of God, atheism violates the canons of rational belief no less than theism. Atheists who regard their attitude toward God as superior to that of theists are mistaken.

As long as you acknowledge the difference between what you believe as articles of faith and what you believe on rational grounds, philosophers are not going to critique your position. But when articles of faith are permitted to affect public policy debates, then the situation may become serious. The absence of objective standards for articles of faith means that virtually anyone can believe virtually anything as articles of faith, including contrary and even contradictory beliefs. There is no prospect for rational public policies under those conditions.

## Approved Motivations

The obsession of the Christian right with abortion, stem-cell research, and cloning appears to have deep roots in its preoccupation with human sexuality. According to its public proponents, there are only two reasons for humans to have sex, which are procreation and recreation. Procreation is ordained by God, recreation is not. Hence, if sex is not motivated by a desire to procreate, it contravenes God's will and becomes an animalistic exercise. It follows from this framework that contraception and birth control—and even sex education and planned parenthood—are unacceptable to them and in the eyes of God. The Bush administration has catered to their preferences by undermining the Constitutional separation of church and state thorough 'faith-based initiatives', and by withholding US funding for the United Nations and undermining its efforts to bring contraception and birth control to third world countries.

The problem is not simply that the existence of God cannot be proven but that there is no end of sources claiming to speak for God. The division of intercourse between humans into reproduction or recreation, for example, affords a nice case of the fallacy of the specious bifurcation, in which two alternatives are juxtaposed and treated as though they were mutually exclusive and jointly exhaustive. Think about the third alternative: sexual relations as an expression of affection between adults in a loving relationship. The rhetorical condemnation of non-reproductive sex loses much of its impact as soon as we acknowledge that there may be a place for sex which is not intended to be reproductive, yet does not fall into the category of merely recreational. Not all non-reproductive sex is therefore reckless sex, even if right-wing evangelists talk as if it were. In relation to the expression of affection between adults, after all, there is a role for contraception and birth control.

It's therefore stunning to discover that the Christian right has taken an extreme stand against a major scientific innovation that protects girls and young women from cervical cancer. A federal panel has recommended that all girls and women between the ages of eleven and twenty-six should receive this vaccine, Gardasil. According to an article in the *New York Times* (Harris 2006), it "protects against cancer and genital warts by preventing infection from four strains of the human papillomavirus, the most common sexually transmitted diseases."

The practical problems that attend this vaccine concern its complex schedule of inoculations (three shots over six months), its cost (at $360, among the most expensive ever), and opposition from religious groups (especially those that advocate abstinence). Even though it has been hailed as a 'breakthrough for women's health' in combating hundreds of thousands of deaths from cancer each year and the federal government is expected to contribute to offsetting its expense, a powerful lobby stands poised to oppose it and to take an aggressive stand to defeat it.

According to Gene Gerard (2006), even though Gargasil seems to be about one hundred percent effective in guarding against cervical cancer, "many conservative organizations oppose it on the grounds that it *might* promote promiscuity among adolescent girls. Now that the FDA has approved the vaccine, conservatives are already working feverishly to limit or prevent its use." It would be difficult to imagine a more clear-cut case in which acceptance of religious doctrines contravenes scientific progress and the health and welfare of women. Does anyone seriously believe that a young woman will be motivated to have sex because she knows of the existence of a vaccine that protects her from cervical cancer and genital warts? This appears to be on a par with the attitude displayed by the religious right in relation to abortion as though a young woman would become pregnant in order to have an abortion. These policies provide striking support for the inference that the religious right is not just opposed to abortion but actually obsessed with sex, not really pro-life but anti-sex.

## 5.1 *Flag Burners, Hookers, and Pot-Heads*

Politics and morality have an uneasy relationship, because while most Americans like to think they're moral, their understanding of principles of morality is typically shallow and insubstantial. A distinction has to be drawn here between 'popular morality' and 'true morality', because most

Americans would take strong exception to the idea that they might not be moral, even if they discriminate on the basis of race, religion, ethnicity, or sex. They do not understand that morality entails treating everyone with respect and never treating persons merely as means. That deeper lesson somehow has never quite caught on. Consequently, in the popular mind, practices like flag burning, smoking pot, and prostitution are commonly assumed to be immoral. Beliefs that are widespread need not be true.

Republicans repeatedly accuse Democrats of being a party of special interests, including blacks and gays, feminists and unionists, the poor and the homeless. Exactly what the Republicans represent apart from other special interests is not entirely clear. What is clear is that the Republican Party is the party of the rich. But, because the rich are small in number, their candidates cannot be elected without receiving support from other segments of society with whom they have practically nothing in common. The party uses social issues to harvest votes from the non-rich by fanning the flames of emotions over abortion, school prayer, and burning the flag. Since the Supreme Court has ruled that abortions are legal and no one—not even the government!—can stop any one from praying—in school or out—these are all implausible planks for a national party. Does anyone think that the rich do not arrange abortions for their daughters when they incur unwanted pregnancies? But the non-rich still rally to their cause by the millions. The GOP has run up an impressive string of victories.

## A Burning Issue?

Because burning a flag is the proper method for disposing of a flag, it is not really flag burning that provokes such heated opposition but burning the flag as an act of protest against policies of the government of which you disapprove. I would have thought it was far better to burn a symbol of the country than the country itself, but that is not how these social conservatives see it. Only about six flags are actually burned in any given year, so it is not much of a problem, and it brings a lot of voters to their booths. The non-rich, who favor school prayer and oppose abortions and burning the flag, periodically join with the rich, who really couldn't care less, to elect candidates to public office. Since their non-rich supporters are large in number while their rich supporters are few, they are thereby compelled to adopt positions in which they do not believe to promote the interests of the rich, which they want to advance. But they do this only 'officially', as a sop to gain support. Which is why Republicans so often disavow their platform!

Imagine if you wanted to maximize the flag-burning issue to motivate your base. Surely the best possible way to secure that objective would be by arranging for a very close vote. And, indeed, it could not have been closer in 2006, when a sixty-six-to-thirty-four vote left the amendment just one vote sort of the sixty-seven needed to send it to the states for ratification (Hulse 2006). There are signs that the American people are catching on. Even Gary Trudeau ran a sequence in Doonesbury (Trudeau 2006), where an aide explains to President Bush, "Sir, the reason we're not getting a bounce from flag-burning is that it hardly ever happens anymore." He continues, "We may need to stage something. You know. Pay some kid to burn a flag in a public place." And the President replies, "Yes . . . I like that! Find someone who has a beef with the government, maybe someone who has just been fired." Doonesbury fans know what happened next. Humor often has its roots in truth.

## Leaving Prostitutes Alone

No doubt, the strongest argument against prostitution is its alleged immorality; otherwise, it could be viewed simply as an exchange of services for money. If this means no more than that most people tend to believe prostitution is immoral, that appears to be correct. But if this is taken to mean prostitution actually is immoral, then an argument is required. Believing something isn't enough to make it true. That the Sun revolves around a flat and motionless Earth is part and parcel of false beliefs that once were also widely held. Some people probably believe it to this day. That an activity is presently illegal does not establish that it is immoral, any more than its morality guarantees its legality. We know slavery has been both legal and illegal, even though slavery is immoral, if any action is. We also know that the duty to always treat others with respect does not entail never treating others as means.

The relationship between employers and employees, for example, is clearly one in which employers use their employees as a means to conduct a business and make profits, while employees use their employment as a means to make a buck and earn a living. Within a context of mutual respect, this is moral conduct. When employers subject their employees to unsafe working conditions, excessive hours, or poor wages, however, the relationship becomes exploitative and immoral, which can also occur when employees do not perform their duties, steal from their employers, or abuse the workplace. Similar considerations apply to doctors and patients, students and faculty, or ministers and congregations, which explains our dismay when such relationships are violated.

There appear to be no inherent reasons prostitution should not qualify as moral so long as hookers and their tricks treat one another with
respect. Hookers are immoral when they do not provide the services
agreed upon, steal their tricks' money, or expose them to venereal disease,
while johns are immoral when they do not pay for services rendered,
engage in physical abuse, or infect their professional providers with disease. Respect works both ways round. Even when prostitution happens to
be legal, immorality can enter by means of other relationships. When hus-
bands or wives commit adultery and thereby betray their commitments
to each other, they are not displaying respect for their spouses and are acting immorally. But that remains the case apart from any commercial
aspects. Prostitution has been described as the world's oldest profession.
Marriage itself was once described, by George Bernard Shaw, as legal
prostitution.

The problems that arise relative to prostitution are generated largely
by its illegality, not by its immorality. In those locales where prostitution
is legal, such as regions in West Las Vegas, women can freely choose this
line of work without the intervention of pimps, who sometimes would
turn them into sexual slaves. When prostitution is illegal, no doubt, the
consequences are often immoral both for hookers and their tricks alike.
During his days as Governor of Minnesota, Jesse Ventura observed, "If it's
legal, then the girls could have health checks, unions, benefits, anything
any other worker gets, and it would be far better" (Grobel 1999). As long
as men and women want to have sex and cannot locate suitable partners
any other way, prostitution seems likely to persist. The problem with
prostitution is not its immorality. The problem is to handle it properly.

## The New Prohibition

The situation relative to pot, if anything, would seem to be even more
clear-cut. Our nation is saturated with drugs, from aspirin, Advil, Tylenol,
and Claritin to cigarettes, chewing tobacco and even cigars. You cannot
read a newspaper or a magazine, watch television or listen to the radio
without encountering a plethora of advertising for drugs promising to
reduce weight, promote hair growth, or help overcome erectile dysfunc-
tion. The Noble Experiment banning alcohol, which endured from 1920 to
1933 with the enactment and then repeal of the Eighteenth Amendment
by the Twenty-First, had devastating consequences for America.
Prohibiting the manufacture, transportation, transportation, and sale of
alcoholic liquors for beverage purposes produced effects that parallel those
we are encountering today from prohibiting the sale of marijuana.

The profound and still enduring effects of prohibition, as Peter McWilliams (1996) has observed, include (1) generating disrespect for the law, (2) eroding respect for religion, (3) creating organized crime, (4) corrupting law enforcement, the court system, and politics, (5) overburdening the police, the courts, and the penal system, and (6) harming millions of persons financially, emotionally, and morally. It also (7) caused physical harm, because safe alcoholic beverages were not then available, (8) changed the drinking habits of the country for the worse, (9) made cigarette smoking a national habit, (10) inhibited the treatment of drinking problems, (11) produced a new category of immorality, and (12) consumed vast financial resources that might have been better used to support education, eradicate disease, and feed the homeless.

Some of these effects are especially intriguing. Because Prohibition was promoted by evangelists and others who wanted to control how other people choose to live their lives, the failure of Prohibition was interpreted as God's failure, especially in the eyes of those who think everything that happens happens in accord with God's will. If God wanted Prohibition to succeed, after all, surely Prohibition would have been a success. Moreover, the cost of this social experiment may be rather difficult to calculate, but McWilliams has estimated that it had to have run into the billions of dollars at a time when the average worker at Ford Motor Company made five dollars a day. "In addition to this cost," McWilliams remarks, "let's not forget the taxes on alcohol the government lost because of Prohibition, and the profit denied honest business people and diverted into the hands of organized crime." Prohibition was costly for the nation.

The situation with respect to pot appears to be precisely the same if not worse. Every consequence that attended Prohibition now attends the 'New Prohibition'. Many authorities say that marijuana is less addicting than nicotine and less harmful to health than alcohol. Yet cigarettes and alcohol are not illegal: their use is regulated, their quality is controlled and their sales are taxed, thereby drastically reducing or even completely nullifying the effects attending Prohibition. The arguments that pot use leads to the use of stronger drugs appears to be a red herring. This claim trades upon a simple equivocation because, while it is true that use of marijuana can lead to using stronger drugs, it is false that smoking marijuana always leads to the use of stronger drugs. Those who use stronger drugs usually have smoked marijuana, but they typically also smoked cigarettes, consumed alcohol, and drank milk. So should drinking milk be a crime?

The strongest opposition to the legalization of marijuana comes from self-appointed religious figures who consider themselves to be the custodians of morality, cowardly politicians who are unwilling to address controversial issues with candor, and the liquor industry, which does not want competition from those who want to smoke their high rather than drink it. Even the effects upon health appear to favor pot over booze. George Pataki, Governor of New York, has granted clemency to four first-time offenders who were serving long prison terms under New York's harsh drug laws. But there are hundreds of thousands more in prisons across the country. The toll in human life over the casual use of recreational drugs staggers the imagination. Uneven enforcement of the law has been scandalous. Lives are ruined over the recreational use of pot. And the lack of evenhandedness is morally outrageous.

Anthony Lewis of the *New York Times* has observed that operating costs for prisons, overflowing with non-violent prisoners, came to about fifty billion dollars in 2000. This cost could be drastically reduced by legalizing the use of pot. Our current policies are so completely ineffectual that even Drug Czar General Barry R. McCaffrey has proposed a more humane approach integrating drug testing and treatment.

I do not want to encourage the widespread use of drugs, but drugs are not going to go away. The drug cartels have expanded and flourished because demand for drugs exceeds the legal supply. When marijuana is legal, its use can be regulated, its quality can be controlled, and its sale can be taxed. Profits from pot will stay out of the hands of organized criminals. Crime and its associated costs will also drop dramatically. We know those who ignore the past are destined to relive it. Surely we can do better.

## 5.2  *Are Corporations Inherently Immoral?*

When former Enron chief executive, Kenneth Lay, now deceased, declined to testify before Congress regarding the apparent fraud and deception being practiced by his company, whose discovery led to its collapse, that profoundly troubled many of our elected representatives. According to the *Duluth News Tribune* (4th February, 2002), Senator Byron Dorgan (D, ND), for example, observed, in response to new disclosures, "It is almost a culture of corruption," where "Once you start peeling away the layers of this onion, it starts to look pretty ugly." The especially troubling question remarks such as these may raise in the minds of Americans is the possibility that corruption might be inherent to corporations.

If corporations are inherently corrupt, then we should have every reason to expect that this Enron may be followed by many other Enrons and that there is really no good reason to suppose that the situation should get better on its own. Indeed, the thought has crossed more than one rational mind that, if corporations as prominent as this one have been able to exert such vast influence in political and economic affairs, then perhaps the only reason we haven't heard of more cases of this kind—apart from the occasional savings and loan scandal, for example—has been our ignorance, where we haven't known because the press has failed to keep us informed.

The reasons, however, may run deeper than that. One problem that has arisen within this context has been a matter of understanding what the word 'corporation' should be understood to mean. The alternatives range from that of a nexus of contracts to a person, where the first reflects a function of corporations (to enter into contracts) and the second a legal fiction (since a business is not a person). A place to start to come to grips with this problem is the dictionary, which offers the following conceptions:

> **(D1) corporation** = df 1 a legal entity, consisting usually of a group of
> people who have a charter granting it perpetual life, that is
> invested with many of the legal powers given to individuals: a
> corporation may enter into contracts, by and sell property, etc. 2
> a group of people, as the mayor and aldermen of an incorpo-
> rated town, legally authorized to act as an individual. 3 any of the
> political and economic bodies forming a corporative state, each
> being composed of the employers and employees in a certain
> industry, profession, etc. 4 a large, prominent belly. (*Webster's
> New World Dictionary*, Third College Edition, 1988)

Imagine my surprise to discover that, contrary to my sincere belief that corporations are not persons, there are definitions, such as 4 above, according to which a part of a person can qualify as a corporation, especially since I had never before thought of myself from that point of view! The evidence in my case may be indisputable, but the sense at stake here is not 4 but 1, which identifies corporations with a group of persons organized for the conduct of business by entering into contracts, which assigns the function (entering into contracts) with those who exercise it (the owners).

The owners of corporations are not always the same as their officers or employees, except in cases in which the officers or employees own stock in the company. So a rather important distinction must therefore be drawn between 'stockholders' as the owners of the company, who may receive dividends, and 'stakeholders' as those persons or other entities having interests that may be affected by its conduct of business, for better or for worse. That includes employees, customers, creditors, and suppliers as well as stockholders, not to mention the community, the environment, and the world.

Just to sharpen our focus and avoid misunderstanding, the conception of corporation that appears to matter within this context can be captured by the following definition:

> **(D2) corporation** = df a legal entity consisting of an arrangement of people and property (roles and assets) interacting together for the purpose of conducting business by a nexus of contracts.

Although this definition may appear to be neutral with regard to the question before us, it fails to take into account the historical context of the times. As Marjorie Kelly (2001), has astutely observed, the standard conception of corporations—the prevailing paradigm within American society—accepts the crucial principle that "the only social responsibility of the corporation is to make a profit," which was initially enunciated by a Nobel Laureate in Economics, Milton Friedman.

Lest we not recognize the importance of this principle, Kelly elaborates its meaning:

> In corporate society, good is what is in the interest of stockholders. That is the primary criterion of morality. It means the corporation has the right to do financial violence to its employees or the environment (conducting massive layoffs, clear-cutting forests), or to attack other corporations (brutal competition, hostile takeovers), if that increases the wellbeing of the ruling tribe, the stockholders.

According to Kelly, prominent philosophers, including Karl R. Popper, have characterized what he calls "the totalitarian theory of morality" as maintaining that "good is what is in the interest of my group; or my tribe; or my state." Thus, such states, for example, are permitted to attack other states, or to do violence to their own citizens, if it benefits the ruling tribe. Or, alternatively, such corporations are permitted to attack other corporations, or to do violence to their own employees, if it benefits the stockholders. These states and corporations are inherently immoral as limited utilitarian entities.

The conclusion that corporations are inherently immoral appears very plausible, but it might be a good idea to investigate the matter further to ascertain whether or not corporations can be moral, in which case they are not necessarily inherently corrupt. If we assume the prevailing paradigm of corporations as profit maximizing entities, then since profits are generated as the difference between net income (as a function of prices for products or for services) and net costs (of producing those products or services—schematically, where profits equal prices minus costs), the principle of profit maximization implies the obvious desirability of inflating prices and deflating costs.

Costs themselves include, among others, those of natural resources, human labor, and taxes. To increase profits, therefore, at least three broad avenues of approach are available related to decreasing costs, namely: (a) decrease the cost of natural resources; (b) decrease the cost of human labor; and (c) decrease the cost of (local, state, and federal) taxes. Alternatively, increase prices to the optimal point where sales produce maximal profits (where the term 'profits' should properly be construed broadly to include such forms of profit as retained earnings, stock options, reinvestments in companies, and such).

The modes of operation that tend to maximize profits thus include (a) decreasing the cost of natural resources by, for example, (i) exploiting the environment, (ii) converting public land to private use, and (iii) evading the expenses of pollution cleanup or costs of environmental restoration; (b) decreasing the cost of human labor by, for example, (i) paying minimal wages, (ii) offering minimal benefits (health coverage, dental plans, and such), and (iii) opposing the organization or diminishing the influence of labor unions that engage in collective bargaining.

Alternatively, (c) decrease the cost of taxes, for example, by (i) resisting paying corporation taxes, (ii) seeking to reduce income tax rates and (iii) attempting to abolish inheritance taxes; or (d) increase the price of your product, for example, by (i) reducing competition, (ii) promoting monopolies, and (iii) manipulating markets (by contriving shortages, disseminating misinformation, and the like). These techniques are morally acceptable to corporations because, as limited utilitarian entities, they are obligated to consider the consequences for no one but themselves. The consequences of their acts for others simply do not matter.

The situation is so drastic that corporations operating as limited utilitarian entities can even resist supporting the social safety net that has been developed since the days of The New Deal, including unemployment insurance, workmen's compensation, Social Security, Medicare, Medicaid, and similar programs, which tend to defeat profit maximization for at least three reasons: (1) they increase the cost of (local, state, and federal) taxation; (2) they create alternatives to low paying, menial jobs; and (3) they thereby empower the workforce with options.

The current trend toward globalization appears to extend the reach of American corporations around the world, where the potential benefits are enormous as a new form of (or a new name for) colonialism and imperialism, for example, by (1) reducing the cost of natural resources; (2) reducing the cost of labor; and (3) reducing the cost of (local, state, and federal) taxation. Thus, it should come as no surprise that the diminution of sweatshops in the United States should be taking place with a commensurate increase in sweatshops elsewhere in the world!

When their conduct is controlled by the principle of maximizing profits, corporations are inherently corrupt. The problem results from the operation of corporations on the basis of Friedman's principle rather than from the definition of corporations themselves. Consequently, it may be said that corporations are inherently *amoral*, which means that they can, but are not obligated to, operate on the basis of principles of morality that involve treating other parties with respect. The situation can be changed, therefore, only by adopting a different paradigm than the prevailing corporate paradigm.

Kelly, for example, suggests that corporate responsibilities should be redefined to maximize benefits, not merely to stockholders, but to stakeholders, where the responsibilities of corporations include taking into account the consequences of their actions for the parties that they affect by not violating their rights. From a moral point of view, this is analogous to abandoning limited utilitarianism and adopting deontological principles as binding on corporations in their relations with stakeholders and only seeking to maximize profits to an extent consistent with deontological morality. This represents a change in corporate paradigms.

The stakeholders, remember, include every party with interests that are affected by the actions of the corporation, that is, which is causally affected, for better or for worse, by its mode of operation, including employees, customers, suppliers, and stockholders, but also the community, the environment, and the world. This approach forsakes short term gains for long term planning, where decisions are made taking into account the answers to questions such as the following three:

- How do corporate actions affect the quality of life of employees?

- How do corporate actions affect sustainability over the long run?

- How do corporate actions affect the survival of the human species?

Such a change represents a shift toward corporations that serve the public good and do not merely promote private greed, as we have seen in the case of Enron.

# 5.3 *Corporatism as American-Style Fascism*

The nature of fascism deserves far more discussion than it has heretofore received. No doubt, the word 'fascism' itself can be used as an emotionally laden description serving as a convenient label that circumvents rational discourse instead of promoting it. It would be irresponsible of a professor of logic and critical thinking to use this word without defining it. Because it is a concept that Americans increasingly need to understand, let's begin with *Webster's New World Dictionary*, Third College Edition (1988), as follows:

> fascism: 1 the doctrines, methods, and movements of the Fascists; 2 a system of government characterized by rigid one-party dictatorship, forcible suppression of opposition, private economic enterprise under centralized government control, belligerent nationalism, racism, and militarism, etc.: first instituted in Italy in 1922 3 a) a political movement based on such policies b) fascist behavior (see Nazi).

An obvious question is the extent to which the candidates of the right represent the interests of the military-industrial complex President Eisenhower warned us about. It ought to be obvious to everyone that George W. Bush and his coterie represent the interests of the big corporations. The form of collusion between government and corporations known as 'corporate welfare' is only a most blatant abuse of the government to benefit the rich and the powerful. The government should act on behalf of all of the people, not merely on behalf of special interests.

The problem is that, without big government to oppose them, big corporations use people merely as mechanisms to produce profit without respecting them as human beings. Does anyone think that Firestone and Ford would ever have considered recalling their products, no matter how defective, were it not for the influence of our government? When governments are controlled by corporations, the forces of fascism thrive and flourish. That is the problem—*the central problem*, I submit—confronting us in this day and age. We verge on fascism. We must understand it.

Fascist tendencies are most obviously evident in ongoing activities that deny voters the right to have their votes counted, rights that are properly clarified by the courts of Florida, of Ohio, and of the United States. When the appointment of electors subverts the rule of law, corrupts the judicial process, and undermines the integrity of the voting process, it strains our faith in democracy. This kind of abuse assumes novel forms when electronic voting machines under the control of private corporations with commitments to one party are permitted to count the votes. As Stalin observed, it doesn't matter who casts the votes. What matters is who counts them. The G.O.P. can count.

It promotes the interests of fascism to weaken and belittle the judicial system, because it represents a barrier against the abuse of citizens, who are now valued only as consumers, as sources of profit. Everyone has a value, within this scheme of things, which turns out to be more or less equal to our own net worth. The aim of big corporations is to separate fools from their money all of the time and ordinary folks from their money most of the time. Absent government regulation, the rest of us must fend for ourselves.

For similar reasons, it serves the ends of fascism to abuse and malign the role of attorneys, especially trial lawyers, as though they were not indispensable elements of the system of checks and balances that keeps the country strong and constrains some of its most powerful forces from exerting disproportionate influence. 'Tort reform', which would impose limits upon awards imposed against corporations, reflects another aspect of a fascist program. And it strangles the resources available to trail lawyers to support the other party.

Every American ought to pause and ask where we, as a country, are going. There have been times in our history when we experienced a certain moral clarity about the world and its affairs, which, alas!, appears to be lost amidst seemingly endless mind-numbing warnings of terrorist threats of one kind or another and the necessity to surrender our civil liberties for increased security. What was it was about fascism and communism, for example, that made them so diametrically opposed to our own nation's principles? How can this President claim to be expanding democracy and freedom abroad while concurrently constricting democracy and freedom at home?

There are three basic issues that define the difference between the totalitarian states and the democratic nations, which concern, first, their tendency toward world domination; second, their government by secrecy; and, third, their control through fear. Our sense of righteousness and moral superiority has derived from our own opposition to these practices, which was rooted in our own traditions of Constitutional government, democratic procedure, and the rule of law. But things are changing. Even the average American seems to realize that things are not quite right.

Consider, for example, the tendencies toward world domination exemplified by Nazis and Communists. Hitler, Stalin, and Mussolini were demonized in part because of their willingness to engage in territorial aggression, changing governments at will, and the assassination of foreign leaders. They were condemned in part because of a blatant disregard for the principles of international law, for violating treaties, for substituting the rule of men for the rule of law. But are we as a nation currently doing any better? Pat Robertson, who poses as a religious leader, makes an appeal for the assassination of Hugo Chavez, the popular leader of Venezuela, who has been elected twice by large margins, and the government of the United States stands mute.

The President of the United States makes a verbal attack upon Iran, Iraq, and North Korea—the "Axis of Evil"—the centerpiece of his State of the Union address and is met with nothing but praise. He subsequently declares the unilateral right of the United States to launch 'pre-emptive attacks' upon other nations if we believe that they are contemplating actions contrary to our own national interests. His Secretaries of State and of Defense actively campaign against the establishment of a World Criminal Court! And the Vice President of the United States argues *against* a Senate ban on torture!

The notion that the US has the right to bring about 'regime change' around the world when it suits our interests has taken a hold upon the imagination of Americans to the extent that we seldom ask whether such actions are even remotely in accordance with international law. We abrogate international agreements, including the Kyoto Accords and the ABM treaty, without consideration for their long-term consequences regarding global warming or their short-term implications for destabilizing the nuclear balance.

We are so preoccupied with threats to our safety that we do not bother to ask whether they might be more imaginary than real. Until the State of the Union speech, Iran had been tending toward more moderate domestic policies, North Korea had been exploring peace talks with South Korea, and Iraq had not engaged in acts of terrorism for at least ten years, according to our own CIA! Yet George W. Bush simply lumped them together as potential targets of pre-emptive strikes and as obvious candidates for regime change. No wonder the rest of the world cringes at the ascension of an American President who appears to have so little regard for the rest of the world!

This administration discussed its plans to insert Special Forces into Iraq, which was a sovereign nation, suggesting that, were Saddam Hussein to be killed in the process, it would not violate the Congressional constraints on political assassinations of foreign leaders, because it would be done in self-defense. The invasion of a sovereign nation by military force and the execution of its leader are justified as acts of 'self-defense'! We seem to have entered an arena where black is white, bad is good, and false is true. George Orwell had it right, but his predictions are being realized more than twenty years after 1984.

We reserve unto ourselves the right to decide when our national interest is at stake, which increasingly appears to be related to the amount of oil that can be found there. From Afghanistan to Iraq and even Venezuela, the politics of oil trump the practice of democracy. We have demonstrated willingness to engage in territorial aggression, to change governments at whim, and to assassinate foreign leaders. Precisely why we are entitled to a sense of moral superiority becomes increasingly difficult to surmise.

The administration's behavior at home has been equally appalling. Government by secrecy has reached a high plateau when the President of the United States can keep official documents and records from the hands of historians and scholars at the stroke of a pen; when a 'secret government' can be formed in the absence of consultation with even the highest ranking members of Congress; and when the nation's energy policy can be fashioned without allowing the public to even know the names of those consulted! If the people are not allowed to know the foreign policy of the United States, how can they possibly know if they support it? The situation is intolerable.

The press appears to have little interest in keeping this nation free or in thinking about the propriety of the administration's actions. That George Bush and Dick Cheney should want to conceal the identity of those who are dictating the nation's policies with regard to energy should come as no surprise, since this is a government of, by, and for corporations, especially companies with names like 'Enron', 'Harken', and 'Halliburton'. Perhaps they don't need to tell us who runs the government because we already know. Perhaps the American people have the government they deserve.

That Bush should want to withhold records from the Reagan administration that would almost certainly reveal that his father was the point man on Iran-Contra, in which we, the United States, traded arms for hostages with Iran and influenced our own election, may also be unsurprising. But surely every American ought to react with alarm at the creation of a secret government operating at 'undisclosed locations', where we appear to be moving far beyond the practices of most totalitarian states.

As though more evidence were needed, the administration has been apprehending, incarcerating, and interrogating persons, some American citizens, whom it charges with vague acts as nonmilitary combatants while denying them the right to legal representation. Indeed, neither the number nor the names of these prisoners are being made available to the public under the guise of undefined threats to 'national security'. We are abusing and blatantly violating our most fundamental principles of due process, some of which, such as habeas corpus, date from *Magna Carta* of 1215.

The administration has shown a remarkable lack of interest in the causes of 9/11. After all, if we actually knew why the United States was being subjected to attack, it might help us to understand what we can do about it. But that has not been the approach of Bush and Cheney, who have actively opposed inquiries by Congress. In the past, blue-ribbon commissions have been created—by FDR within eleven days of the attack on Pearl Harbor, by LBJ within seven days of the assassination of JFK. But not in this case.

The day that Arlen Specter (R-PA) reported that the administration did not merely have "vague warnings" or a "series of dots" that needed to be corrected, but actual "blueprints" of the terrorists' plans to attack the World Trade Center, Bush announced his plan for reorganizing the government by the creation of a new Office of Homeland Security. This sweeping change would bring together a large number of functions from the Secret Service to the Coast Guard, but not the FBI or the CIA.

Anyone who actually thinks that agency-shuffling is going to enhance government efficiency does not understand the desperation of the situation we are in. Coping with terrorism requires timely actions based upon current information. This entity by design has no intelligence capability of its own but is dependent upon the FBI and the CIA for its information. These agencies, by the way, are the same agencies that failed to predict these terrorist attacks or the fall of the Soviet Union.

Moreover, they have been notoriously territorial and unwilling to share information among themselves. By the time the FBI and CIA have figured it out and decided whether or not they are going to share information with each other, much less the Office of Homeland Security, the terrorist attacks they are ostensibly attempting to prevent may have already taken place. There is at least as much reason to expect this outcome as any alternative. But the situation is really much worse.

Bush insisted the 170,000 employees who are staffing this new office have no civil service protection so they are vulnerable to being hired and fired at will. He claimed that this would enhance efficiency, but his true motives appear have been far more sinister. Without civil service protection, those who work in these offices are now vulnerable to threats of firing if they do not co-operate with their bosses, even to the extent to having to implement policies with which they disagree and consider to be illegal or immoral.

This is control by intimidation. Bush has shown his hand by specifically asking that 'whistle-blower' protections be weakened for this new department. He has asked for the authority to shift funding from one branch to another, thereby usurping the role of the legislative branch in making funding determinations. Bush's 'Office of Homeland Security' in turn creates the core of a new 'Office of National Security', as we make our way toward a more compete realization of our new fascist state.

Whistle blowing requires great moral courage and the assumption of responsibility for your actions. It deserves to be encouraged. Bush, however, has taken precisely the opposite tack, even to the extent of threatening to veto entire bills when they do not incorporate the specific provisions he desires. That, I believe, would be a good idea, just as the demise of the Attorney General's plan to create a citizen network of spies has temporarily restrained our headlong rush toward totalitarian government.

I am not the only one to believe that Bush and his cronies are taking advantage of a national catastrophe to promote a reckless agenda that encompasses territorial aggression, governmental secrecy, and control through fear under the banner of patriotism. And it becomes increasingly difficult to identify exactly what it is that differentiates the United States from the fascist and communist nations we have historically opposed. When we look in the mirror, we are finding the enemy is us.

The Bush administration has now promulgated its plans for world domination. Under the title of 'The National Security Strategy of the United States' (*New York Times*, 20th September, 2002), this approach betrays our past heritage as the moral leader of the civilized world and expends our military power for the purpose of promoting our own national self-interest, regardless of the consequences for the rest of the world, in a new form of American imperialism. Its origins are rooted in a study written and published in September 2002, by the Project for the New American Century, a neo-conservative think tank, which lays out the case for US world domination.

The administration's thirty-three-page document, which is available on-line via the *New York Times*, was submitted to Congress in response to a law passed in 1986 that requires such an assessment from each President. It adopts the most aggressive foreign policy in the history of the United States by abandoning non-proliferation treaties in favor of 'counter-proliferation', which includes scrapping the ABM treaty to undertake the construction of our own missile defense systems, and emphasizing our right to 'strike first' at those who would threaten American interests, which the administration takes to be preeminent: whenever US interests are at stake, there will be no compromise.

As David Sanger explains, while the Clinton administration empha-sized reliance upon and enforcement of international treaties—the 1972 ABM Treaty, the Comprehensive Test Ban Treaty, and the Kyoto environ-mental accords, for example—this document 'celebrates' the decision to abandon the ABM treaty, because it imposed constraints upon American efforts to build a missile defense system of its own. The expectation imposed on countries in Kyoto to reduce their $CO_2$ emissions are now displaced by targets, where meeting them becomes merely voluntary. And it rejects the new International Criminal Court, whose jurisdiction, it claims, does not extend to US citizens, no matter what atrocities against humanity they may have committed.

## The Corruption of Limited Utilitarianism

Even though this document is couched in language that expresses appre-ciation for the UN, the WTO, and NATO, it emphasizes the special status of the US as the world's only superpower and baldly asserts that the President has no intention of allowing foreign nations to complete with the US in military power. This document makes it obvious the US sup-ports multilateral approaches to problem solving only when that happens to coincide with US interests, where the US reserves the right to strike first whenever it perceives its national interests are at stake. Its underlying premise appears to be that, because the US has the power to impose its interests, it has the right to do so.

The ancient doctrine that 'Might makes Right' has been repudiated by every student of moral theory, except, it would appear, the present admin-istration. The reason for entities like the UN and the WTO is supposed to be that differences in military and economic power do not compromise the right of nations to be treated alike in accordance with international law. These new Bush policies are blatant examples of the corrupt moral posture know as 'limited utilitarianism', according to which an action is right for a group when it brings about the greatest benefits for that group, regardless of its consequences for everyone else. As we have discovered, this is the most pernicious of all moral theories, because the actions of a group, such as those of the Nazis, can be far more devastating than those of mere individuals. That is the new American way.

Shallow thinkers sometimes maintain that everyone always acts in his own interest, which exemplifies 'ethical egoism'. But that position trades upon an ambiguity that freshmen are taught to avoid, namely: that between motives just being *our own* motives (and in that sense being 'our interests') and motives being intended to promote our own *self-interest*.

Anytime anyone acts from a sense of loyalty, affection, respect, or duty, especially at the expense of one's time, effort, money, or life, they exemplify the poverty of ethical egoism. The inadequacy of limited utilitarianism ought to be even more conspicuous, insofar as Hitler's Germany, Hirohito's Japan, even Stalin's Soviet Union operated on the basis of the very principles that we are now embracing.

Consider Pearl Harbor. The surprise attack upon naval and marine forces stationed in the Hawaiian Islands would have been morally justifiable under 'The National Security Strategy of the United States'. As Robert B. Stinnett, *Day of Deceit* (2000), has explained, the US undertook a series of actions—including arrangements to use British bases in the Pacific; to use bases and acquire supplies in the Dutch East Indies; to give all possible aid to Chiang Kai-shek; to send a division of heavy cruisers and two divisions of submarines into the Orient; to station the US fleet in the Hawaiian Islands; to insist that the Dutch refuse Japanese requests for economic concessions, especially oil; and to join with the British in an embargo of Japanese trade—to provoke Japan.

The key point is this. All of these actions could have been perceived as threats to the national interests of Japan. Under the auspices of some counterpart 'National Security Strategy of Japan', it would have been perfectly appropriate for Japan to undertake a pre-emptive strike at the perceived threat to its national interests then represented by the United States. Far from being regarded "a date that will live in infamy," 7th December, 1941—consistent with this doctrine—could be remembered as a glorious attempt to uphold the national interests of Japan, an act whose legality and propriety are beyond all question. That the war ended in a fashion that was contrary to its interests is merely an accident of history. Japan did the morally right thing!

The philosophy that underlies the Constitution, the Bill of Rights, and the UN charter, is not limited utilitarianism or even classic utilitarianis', according to which actions that bring about at least as much benefit for everyone as any alternative actions are right. In that case, since actions may not benefit everyone the same—our war on Iraq, for example, may be expected to be very costly for Iraqi civilians as well as for Iraqi soldiers—calculations of right and wrong must be made on the basis of net benefits, where the costs for some are subtracted from the benefits for others. This approach, however, like simple majority rule, can be used to justify the most corrupt acts, such as slave-based societies, when they do not properly take into account personal rights.

The Declaration of Independence declares that Americans have inalienable rights to life, liberty, and the pursuit of happiness. We think that's a pretty good thing, even if the founding fathers did not fully include women and slaves within the scope of the rights it was engaged in enumerating. Those would include the right to vote, for example, or the right to be free from unreasonable search or seizure, or the right to forfeit your life, liberty, or property only after a fair trial by a jury of your peers—something called 'due process'. These are the kind of rights that motivated the UN charter, which advocates universal human rights as rights of every human merely because that person is human. They are rights to which every human is entitled.

These rights create reciprocal duties within the framework of what is known as 'deontological moral theory'. According to this approach, we should always treat other persons as ends—as valuable in themselves—and never merely as means. This implies treating other persons with respect, including acknowledging a duty to respect their rights as human beings. When persons violate the rights of others by treating them merely as means, then they are subject to punishment within the framework of due process as it applies to them. In this case, that implies not acting unilaterally to enforce the national interests of the US but taking into account the rights of other nations and populations, including those of Iraq and of Afghanistan.

Unilateral actions may be morally unobjectionable if one nation poses 'an imminent threat' to another. But Iraq posed no such threat to the US. The existence of entities such as the United Nations and the WTO make the class of cases in which unilateral action is required a narrowly circumscribed class. Indeed, the US courted the UN for support because Iraq had violated sixteen of its resolutions intended to bring about the removal of weapons of mass destruction, while simultaneously maintaining that the policy of the US was to bring about regime change. The US had no right, under international law, to initiate regime change merely because it may find that to be in its national interest, and violations of UN resolutions are not 'terrorist acts'. Its appeals to the UN were merely a technique to conceal violations of international law that the US planned to perpetrate based on its commitment to a corrupt moral theory.

Such unilateral actions even appear to violate our own constitution. As an article in the *Duluth News Tribune* (23rd September, 2002) reports, "The United Nations Charter imposes limitations on declarations of war. The US Senate approved the Charter after World War II as a legally binding treaty." Treaties, under the Constitution, are the supreme law of the land. The abrogation of these treaties by this administration probably qualifies as unconstitutional and might well be considered an impeachable offense. When Bush blatantly disregards this nation's commitments under the Charter, he not only violates international law but also the Constitution of the US. The neo-conservatives despise the UN and would like nothing more than to weaken it.

A policy of pre-emption is inherently destabilizing. Embracing first strikes encourages attacks upon your enemy for perceived threats, real or imagined. Unlike our policies of the past, according to which the US would attack you only if you attacked us first, this new approach functions as an incentive to use 'em or lose 'em. It will inevitably encourage Pakistan to attack India, China to attack Taiwan, North Korea its southern neighbor, and—as things now appear—Iran to attack US forces in the Middle East. In view of our announced objectives, if Saddam had possessed chemical, biological, or nuclear weapons, it would have been immoral for him not to use them against the threat the US posed under the auspices of 'The National Security Strategy of Iraq'!

According to a piece in the *Sunday Herald* (15th September, 2002), Bush planned to attack Iraq and bring about regime change even before he became President. Neil Mackay reports that a master plan to create a global *Pax Americana* that would exceed the dominance over the world exerted by the ancient Roman Empire had already been drafted, The Project for a New American Century (PNAC), with input from Dick Cheney, Donald Rumsfeld, and Paul Wolfowitz, among others. The report is available at newamericancentury.org/publicationsreports.htm. Yet the American press did not inform Americans.

As Mackay explains, this document provides "a blueprint for maintaining global US preeminence, precluding the rise of a great power rival, and shaping the international security order in line with American principles and interests." This approach clearly does not take into account whether such a plan would be beneficial for the rest of the world's population—not even to the extent that it may affect its prospects for survival and reproduction! If every human being has the right to life, liberty, and the pursuit of happiness, however, then the US has an obligation to take into account how actions it might pursue would impact on other nations and the world. It cannot act solely in its own national interest and satisfy the requirements of deontological moral theory.

Among the objectives specified by the PNAC report that are explicit or implied by the new strategic policy of the US are these: maintaining relations with allies as means to promote American global domination; treating 'peace keeping' missions as requiring US rather than UN leadership; doing whatever is necessary to undermine European solidarity if that could rival US preeminence; permanently occupying Iraq, with or without Saddam, to maintain US influence in the Middle East and its control over oil; creating US 'space forces' to control military uses of space; taking steps to ensure US control of cyberspace; continuing to develop our own chemical, biological, and nuclear weapons; and maintaining focus on Syria, Lybia, Iran, and North Korea as dangerous regimes which, over the long run, along with China, are candidates for regime change.

The article concludes with quotes from Tam Dalyell, a Labor MP in the British House of Commons, who says:

> This is garbage from right-wing think tanks stuffed with chicken-hawks—men who have never seen the horror of war but are in love with the idea of war. Men like Cheney, who were draft-dodgers in the Vietnam war. This is a blueprint for US world domination—a new world order of their own making. These are the thought processes of fantasist [those who fantasize, but he may have meant fascist] Americans who want to control the world. I am appalled a British Labour Prime Minister should have got into bed with a crew which has this [low] moral standing.

The overt reason given for opposing the new International Criminal Court, as Bush and Cheney have alleged, it that the United States might become the target of flimsy charges for political purposes by nations that dislike us. But there are more ominous reasons for supposing that we might become parties to suits before this court, such as blatant violations of international law. The US and its ally, Israel, have histories of committing serious crimes against humanity, including terrorism, assassination, and coups. Calling them 'regime changes' does not alter their legal or their moral character. The best reason for opposing the Court, in their eyes, may simply be to keep Bush, Cheney, Rumsfeld, Wolfowitz, and Ariel Sharon free from prosecution and out of prison, where the cumulative evidence suggests they properly belong.

That fascism has come to America becomes increasingly apparent when Bush has imposed his interpretation upon legislation passed by Congress, not once or twice but 750 times, thereby presuming unto himself the functions of the legislative and of the judiciary branches of government. A more conspicuous sign that the US has lost its Constitutional compass would be difficult to arrange. Unless, say, the people of the United States were to awaken to the realization that their President has gone forward with a plan to create a North American Union merging Canada and Mexico with the United States, where national sovereignty and even states' rights no longer matter, without consulting them. Or if, without a single word of discussion or debate in the halls of Congress, he had initiated a series of NAFTA 'super highways', which will turn the US into several zones of commerce, completely transforming the nation for the benefit of corporations. And he may deliberately precipitate a financial crisis to justify abandoning the dollar in favor of the Amero, to benefit not ordinary citizens but the rich and powerful. Short-term profit maximization may in turn promote global warming and the extinction of the species. And that, alas, appears to be where we are heading.

# How Science Can Help
# Public Policy

➦ *Culture enables evolution to incorporate the inheritance of valuable acquired patterns of behavior*

➦ *Science cannot set society's goals but it can help society attain them*

➦ *The Good Society is founded on the deontological principle that every member of society is entitled to the same rights and opportunities as every other*

➦ *Public schools should be secular but not atheistic*

➦ *Members of a moral society must tolerate group differences as well as individual differences*

*Men never do evil so completely and cheerfully as when they do it from religious conviction.* (Pascal, *Pensées*)

$\mathcal{W}$e know that evolution can be envisioned in at least three different ways, namely: as a set of causal mechanisms, including genetic mutation, sexual reproduction, natural selection, genetic drift, sexual selection, group selection, artificial selection, and genetic engineering; as a set of evolutionary explanations, where those mechanisms are applied to specific historical circumstances to explain specific evolutionary events, such as the extinction of the dinosaurs; and as a history of species, which records the emergence and the extinction of various species across time as a consequence of the operation of its causal mechanisms to those historical conditions.

But our conception of the full range of those causal mechanisms must be substantially broadened to encompass the place of culture in evolution. This shift in perspective can be displayed by using simple models of the evolutionary process. Figure 6.1 reflects a rather standard conception of genetic evolution, for which evolution is measured by means of changes in gene frequencies across time, survival and reproduction to perpetuate genes by means of offspring is the motive that dominates behavior, and what transpires subsequent to reproduction—apart from looking after those offspring—has little or no biological significance. The tendency here is to assume that every instance of the same body (phenotype) possesses the same behavioral dispositions, where minor variations affect fitness. In these diagrams, ef1, ef2, . . . stand for environmental factors.

**Figure 6.1** A Model of Genetic Evolution

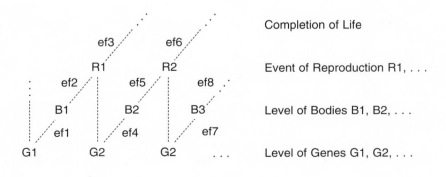

---

153

Even while acknowledging the role of pleiotropic and polygenic effects as a source of variation in phenotypes, the role of cultural contributions to behavior tends to be suppressed either because every member of the species displays similar behavior (the instinctual species) or because the influence of inherited tendencies greatly outweighs that of acquired ones (biological determinism). But, while genes are indeed the units of selection, behavior is the level at which selection occurs; and to the extent to which behavior is affected by culture, the first model appears deficient. The second, however, assumes that similar bodies (phenotypes) can acquire and display different behavioral dispositions, because—even if every instance of a phenotype has the same predispositions to acquire behavioral dispositions, under the same conditions—those conditions, in turn, are subject to a wide range of variation. (Fetzer 2005)

**Figure 6.2** A Model of Gene-Culture Co-Evolution

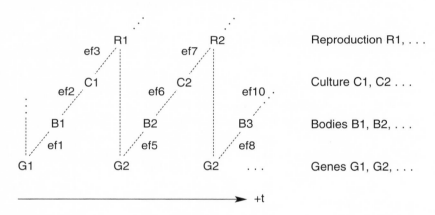

Figure 6.2 goes beyond Figure 6.1 in acknowledging a place for culture in contributing to the survival and evolution of the species by means of causal mechanisms that transcend those admitted by more conventional evolutionary theories, including the role of customs, traditions, and practices that are transient rather than permanent properties of the members of those species, races, or groups. These causal mechanisms are psychological rather than biological in their character, encompassing different forms of learning from classic conditioning to rational criticism as forms of intelligence that are responsive to the current environment, whereby they can acquire dispositions reflective of the latest customs, traditions, and practices in the evolution of memes, which makes gene-culture co-evolution a Lamarckian rather than merely Darwinian process.

# 6.1 *The Morality of Science*

Gene-culture co-evolution does not imply that genetic evolution allows the biological inheritance of acquired characteristics. What gene-culture co-evolution permits is the cultural inheritance of acquired characteristics, encapsulated by the notion that we don't have to re-invent the wheel—or jet propulsion, color television, or digital machines, for that matter.

What gene-culture co-evolutionary theory provides is an evolutionary framework for understanding cultural and evolutionary phenomena as they are instantiated by species whose behavior is not entirely or predominantly instinctual, including especially the higher species. For the study of the behavior of individuals, of groups, and of cultures reflects laws of nature only to the extent to which that behavior is the product of permanent properties.

The permanent properties of neurologically-normal human beings include predispositions to acquire other dispositions under suitable conditions, which include especially predispositions for the acquisition of semiotic abilities in the form of intelligence as mentality of a high order in comparison with other species. The existence of evolved differences between sub-populations supplies a foundation for understanding differences between them, but it does not preclude taking measures to change or improve them. Within democratic societies, however, steps of that kind must be decided by a political process in determining how public resources should be expended in the public interest. Science as such can contribute to the public debate over such issues, but it cannot determine what measures society should undertake.

As Carl G. Hempel (1965) has explained, a distinction must be drawn between value judgments of two kinds, namely: hypothetical (or conditional) and categorical (or unconditional). Hypothetical imperatives concern means that are effective, efficient, or reliable in attaining a certain end, and thus have the form, 'If goal G is to be attained, under conditions of kind C, then means M would be appropriate'. Categorical imperatives, by contrast, apply to and themselves reflect commitments to G. They thus have the form, 'Goal G should be attained'. Hempel remarks that unconditional value judgments of this kind lie beyond what science is able to provide. Science can ascertain whether or not children are happier and better adjusted when they are raised in permissive rather than restrictive environments, but cannot decide whether a society should have happier and better adjusted children.

In this sense, science can contribute to the attainment of the goals of a society by discovering which means are the most efficient, effective, or reliable for the attainment of specific aims, objectives, or goals, but does not decide which aims, objectives, or goals are those of a society. When we study social science research, therefore, it is essential to distinguish

**Table 6.1** Three Theses from *The Bell Curve*

(**T1**) The cognitive elite is getting richer, in an era when everybody else is having to struggle to stay even;

(**T2**) The cognitive elite is increasingly segregated physically from everyone else, in both the workplace and the neighborhood;

(**T3**) The cognitive elite is increasingly likely to intermarry. (Herrnstein and Murray 1996, p. 114)

these reports as descriptive findings about society from prescriptions as to precisely what, if anything, should be done about them. Questions of fact, such as 'Is a cognitive elite emerging within our society?', must be separated from questions of value, such as 'Is the emergence of a cognitive elite within our society a good thing?' Insofar as science is preoccupied with answering questions of fact and not with answering questions of value, moreover, it should be apparent that science cannot dictate the course society should follow.

## 6.2  *Politics and the Good Society*

The process of adopting means that are efficient, effective, or reliable in order to attain specific goals presupposes the availability of relevant findings of the kind that science can provide. Without knowing empirical facts about the emergence of a cognitive elite (the evolution of predispositions toward semiotic abilities, which may differ within sub-populations, and so on), however, it is very difficult to imagine that societies can make rational decisions about the allocation of its resources in the public interest. It appears to be rather ironic that some of the most serious students of group and racial differences, including Rushton and Herrnstein and Murray, have been attacked for pursuing scientific studies of important issues in the absence of knowledge of which appropriate public policies are unlikely to be adopted within our own society (Murray 1996; Rushton 1996).

To offer an illustration, the acquisition of different habits of action and habits of mind as an effect of our life histories strongly affects our capacity to subsume various experiences by means of corresponding concepts. Those with restricted opportunities to learn and to acquire concepts are therefore inhibited from interacting with their environments in ways that might enhance their fitness. A society that wants to benefit all of its members, therefore, should promote their opportunities for diversified experiences that enhance their acquisition of concepts, especially at an early age. Moreover, as Clark Glymour (1998, p. 30) observes, the impact of computers may be different than Herrnstein and Murray suppose, because computers enable people with relatively modest training to perform many tasks "as well [as] or better than those with special talents. It is the great equalizer."

Classic utilitarianism, including principles such as the greatest good for the greatest number, is only compatible with a moral society when it is combined with minority rights. Those principles are not only compatible with a slave-based society but with the behavior of a lynch mob. If the course of conduct that provides the greatest happiness to the greatest number is 'stringing them up', then lynching is a morally justifiable action under those conditions. A good society, by contrast, insists that every citizen be treated with respect, which includes not depriving them of life, liberty, or the pursuit of happiness in the absence of due process. The lynch mob exemplifies the greatest happiness for the greatest number but it affords no protection for individual liberty or for minority rights.

The Good Society must be founded upon deontological principles, where every member of society—rich or poor, black or white, powerful or powerless—is entitled to the same rights and opportunities as every other under the law, which is the kind of framework that the Constitution combined with the Bill of Rights provides. These rights were regarded by our Founding Fathers as endowments bestowed upon us by Our Creator; but it does not require religious belief to recognize the most defensible theory of morality. Indeed, it is part and parcel of understanding that God would have us do what is right because it is right and not merely because he wills it. We must exercise our reason in order to discover what God would have us do, which is the kind of exercise in which we have been engaged here. But we have also reach the point of appreciating that morality does not require religion or even belief in God.

Religion provides a motive for being moral rather than defining morality. Those who believe in an afterlife in which justice will be served—the guilty will go to Hell and the innocent to Heaven—have an inducement to accept injustice in life on Earth. But there are those who would exploit human vulnerability to accept articles of faith. Jim Lobe (2003), for example, lays out the principles advanced by a figure who has exerted profound influence upon key members of the Bush administra-tion. These include the distinction between those who are entitled to rule—and who realize that there is no morality—and those over whom they rule. Leo Strauss feared that the masses would fall into anarchy or nihilism in the absence of belief in religion and therefore endorsed the use of religion to induce false beliefs about morality as mechanisms of control. His views reek of limited utilitarianism, but they have pro-foundly affected the course of recent history. Politics without morality yields corruption.

## 6.3  *Must Science and Religion Conflict?*

None of us has privileged access to the truth in matters of religion. When it comes to belief in God, we all appear to be in the same epistemic quandary, because we have no way to tell for sure whether one or more divine beings even exist, or if they do exist, exactly what they are like. No matter what course history may take, including overpopulation, global pollution, and nuclear war, it can be reconciled with the existence or the non-existence of God. Traditional conceptions envision God as a tran-scendent being completely unlike any natural phenomenon. Scientific inquiries cannot address phenomena that lie beyond the possibility of empirical investigation. Typical beliefs about God are therefore empiri-cally untestable. Answers based on faith do not qualify as knowledge.

Jimmy Stewart starred in a movie, *Harvey*, playing Elwood P. Dowd, an affable alcoholic who had an ongoing relationship with a large but invisible rabbit. While the film was amusing, few would mistake Elwood's belief in Harvey for knowledge. There was no evidence of Harvey's exis-tence except in Elwood's mind. God is also an invisible being, but one that occupies all space and all time. There are many alternative conceptions, of course, including the existence of many gods (polytheism), identifying God with nature (pantheism), and the conception of God as having cre-ated the world and allowing it to run its course (deism), as well as more traditional alternatives. The strongest conception envisions God as an omniscient, omnipotent, and omnibenevolent being, who knows every-thing, can do anything, and wants only good. But the existence of so much misery then becomes a mystery difficult to comprehend.

According to the ethics of belief, atheism is just as immoral as theism. The only morally justifiable position is agnosticism. Anyone can believe anything they want regardless of the evidence, as an article of faith. Fifty percent of the population believe in ghosts, twenty-five percent believe in witches, and programs and films about angels are wildly popular. You can believe in werewolves, vampires, and leprechauns if you like. Just don't mistake your beliefs for knowledge.

Public schools should be secular out of respect for everyone's right to their personal beliefs. But they are not therefore bastions of atheism. The Ten Commandments, organized prayer, and Creationism as science are out of place in public schools, which must practice agnosticism out of impartiality. Those who impose their religious beliefs upon others are acting immorally.

In *Why I Am Not a Christian* (1957), Bertrand Russell has maintained that more people have been slaughtered in the name of religion than from all other deliberate causes combined. This sad state of affairs, which continued unabated to this day, tends to reflect the power of faith and the impotence of reason.

There are hundreds of world religions, denominations, and sects, each of which claims to have privileged access to the truth, and the declared truth differs from one religion, denomination, and sect to another. These beliefs, undoubtedly, cannot all be true, since they bear allegiance to different leaders and texts, different conceptions of God, and different articles of faith. But there has to be an enormous attraction in holding beliefs that, because they transcend experience, cannot be proven false. If one religion promises eternal life to those who take the lives of their religious enemies, who can show them to be in error? For certain groups and times, such beliefs can have adaptive benefits.

A moral society cannot allow some citizens to slaughter other members in the name of God or of atheism. A democratic society cannot allow some religions to have priority over other religions in the education of its members. But that does not preclude the prospect of offering courses on religion in the public school classrooms, provided that they are conducted in ways that are respectful to all points of view.

Creationism should not be taught as science because its hypotheses and theories are not scientific. But Creationism and other religious perspectives might readily be taught, in their varied manifestations, in a course on comparative religions, where students have an opportunity both to explore and to evaluate a broad range of religious alternatives for themselves.

Scientific knowledge will never be complete and we will never know everything there is to know about the beginning of the universe (Rogers 1999; Johnson 1999), the origin of life (Wade 1999; Eschenmoser 1999), the evolution of species (Lemonck and Dorfman 1999; Stevens 1999), or the roots of culture (Wilford 1999a; 1999b). The temptation to deny our ignorance, which is great, by invoking articles of faith, which are abundant, may persist indefinitely. But if we substitute faith for knowledge in matters of this kind, our survival as a species will be in jeopardy. The challenge we confront as a species is doing our best to ensure we do not join the ninety-eight percent of species that have already attained extinction. There are no guarantees that we shall succeed, but forsaking science is not a viable option.

In the final analysis, the members of a moral society must become as tolerant of group differences as they are of individual differences. The underlying problem is not diversity but stereotypes, where persons are treated not as individuals but as instances of preconceptions. Aristotle defined humans as rational animals; others envision us as "the symbolic species" (Deacon 1997) or as "the moral animal" (Wright 1994).

Species able to use symbols qualify as semiotic systems of a high kind, while those that are able to reason qualify as semiotic systems of an even higher kind. Our capacity for criticism qualifies us as semiotic systems of the highest kind. Our aspiration for a moral society, rooted in the ability to compare differences between how things are and how they ought to be, displays it vividly. While our degrees of intelligence and rationality partially distinguish us from other species, our most remarkable trait is the ability to embrace a morality that transcends our biology.

# APPENDIX

# Defining Science

→ *Science looks for natural laws which will explain and predict*

→ *Scientific theories are never quite proved by the evidence, as they always outstrip the evidence in their favor*

→ *There are different conceptions of science: they must all include Popper's idea that science strives to refute its hypotheses*

→ *According to abductivism, the best theory of what science is, traditional Creationism cannot qualify as science as it offers no testable explanations of why things are the way they are*

→ *Insofar as testable scientific hypotheses can be extracted from classic Creationism, they make no reference to God and thus defeat the point of Creationism*

$\mathcal{T}$o argue, as I have done, that Creationism is not science, requires that I try to explain how I conceive of what science is. I will here describe laws of nature, then consider three conceptions of science, and then appraise the scientific standing of three classic Creationist hypotheses.

## 7.1 *What Are Natural Laws?*

The proper relationship between the history of science and the philosophy of science comes to this: that the aim of science can only be ascertained by investigating the history of science, while the methods of science are properly established on the basis of philosophical reflections (Fetzer 1981; 1993). The difference thus displayed is one between 'means' and 'ends'; for although traditional aims of inquiry can be established historically, the most appropriate means for their attainment need not be the same as those we happen to employ. There are no built-in guarantees that the methods employed by many or by most or by all of those who call themselves members of the scientific community are necessarily the most effective, the most efficient or the most reliable to achieve a given goal—even when that goal happens to be the very purpose of scientific inquiry itself.

I shall thus assume that an investigation of the history of science—from classic sources such as van der Waerden's *Science Awakening* and Neugebauer's *Exact Sciences in Antiquity*, on to Kuhn's *Copernican Revolution* and Holton's *Thematic Origins of Scientific Thought*—would establish that science does have its own distinctive objective, namely: the discovery of general principles by means of which the phenomena of experience may be subjected to explanation and to prediction, where these 'general principles' in turn possess the form of scientific theories and of natural laws. Indeed, scientific theories are suitably viewed as sets of laws and definitions that apply to a common domain, thereby permitting the concise depiction of science as aiming at the discovery of natural laws.

Any other activity could be perfectly worthwhile, but it would not be science. Accepting the aim of science to be the discovery of natural laws does not determine which methods are most efficient, effective, or reliable for such a purpose, but it would be widely agreed that the application of those methods presupposes the availability of experiential findings in the form of a (perhaps quite large) set of singular sentences $e$ describing the contents of experience in the form of observations, measurements, or experiments. Thus, given a specific set of alternative hypotheses or theories $h1$, $h2$, ..., $hn$, the philosophical problem becomes that of identifying and justifying principles of inference that would establish which among the alternatives $h1$, $h2$, ..., $hn$ receives the strongest evidential support from the evidence $e$, whether or not that evidence would qualify as conclusive.

Scientific reasoning is characteristically inconclusive, in the sense that the truth of the evidence $e$ does not, as a rule, guarantee the truth of one or more alternative hypotheses $h1$ to $hn$. The reasons are many and varied, ranging from practical limitations that stem from the current availability of technical apparatus, such as electron microscopes and radio telescopes, qualified personnel and suitable funding to inherent limitations arising because the content of any conclusion reached, say, $hi$, characteristically goes beyond the content of the available evidence, $e$. This occurs whenever we draw conclusions about populations on the basis of samples, whenever we make inferences about the future on the basis of our experience in the past and whenever we derive conclusions about non-observables on the basis of observations.

The ultimate source of this tension, however, is the nature of laws of nature. Most theoreticians would agree that laws involve relations between properties, although some would hold out for classes instead. Classes differ from properties insofar as classes are said to be the same when their members are the same, a principle that does not hold true of properties. As Willard Quine has observed,

> classes are the same when their members are the same, whereas it is not universally conceded that properties are the same when possessed by the same objects ... But classes may be thought of as properties if the latter notion is so qualified that properties become identical when their instances are identical. (Quine 1951, p. 120)

Since classes are the same when their members are the same, they are said to be 'completely extensional' entities. No specific conditions need to be satisfied by the members of a class other than that they be collected together or are jointly grouped as members of that class.

An old comb, the square root of $-1$, and the current President of the United States, for example, could be taken to be the three members of a class, even though they might share no—or virtually no—conditions, characteristics, or properties in common, apart from the trivial property of being grouped together as members of this specific class. Some of them do not even qualify as physical things. Quine's phrasing here is exceptionally important within the present context. He says that two classes are the same if they have the same members, but that two properties are the same when they have the same members as long as we take it to be the case that properties are the same when their instances are the same.

He is saying properties can be treated as if they were classes by assumption. Those who make this assumption are 'nominalists', those who deny it 'realists'. On nominalist principles, there can be no difference between properties—however counterintuitive it may appear—when they have the same instances. Thus, since there are no unicorns, vampires, or werewolves, the terms 'unicorn', 'vampire', and 'werewolf' have the same extension, namely, nothing, or, as it is known in logical theory, the empty class (or the 'null' class). It follows on nominalist principles that the properties of being a unicorn, of being a vampire, and of being a werewolf are one and the same property. This is quite an extraordinary result, because normally we would never have confused them.

Not only are unicorns, vampires, and werewolves the same kind of thing, on nominalist principles, given that properties with the same instances have to be identical, but they are also the same kind of thing as numbers that are both odd and even, circles with four sides, and other impossibilia. If the objection arises that circles with four sides and other impossibilia are abstract rather than physical entities, moreover, it invites the rebuttal that, if things can in fact be differentiated on the basis of their properties even when their instances are the same, after all, then surely we can differentiate between unicorns, vampires and werewolves—as we ordinarily do—even when they have the same class of instances!

This issue assumes considerable importance because nominalism supports a theory according to which natural laws merely describe correlations between instances of properties (classes) that happen to occur during the course of the world's history, which thus views sentences that describe them as *extensional*. Realism, by contrast, supports an alternative account according to which there is more to natural laws than mere correlations between instances of properties (classes) that happen to occur during the course of the world's history, which instead views sentences that describe them as *intensional* (Fetzer 1981; 1993). The problem that realists encounter and that nominalists avoid, therefore, is to provide a defensible distinction between correlations that are and are not lawful, while nominalists are compelled to deny there is any distinction to be drawn.

The difference between them can be illustrated in relation to the following columns of property (or class) designators, which might have many instances:

**Table 7.1** Some Properties and Attributes

| R | A |
|---|---|
| red | round |
| wooden | cuckoo-clock |
| gold | melting point of 1064°C |
| polonium [218] | half-life of 3.05 minutes |

No doubt, there is some relative frequency with which things-that-are-red are things-that-are-round, with which things-that-are-wooden are things that-are-cuckoo-clocks, and so forth, as features of the history of the world. Equally clearly, no doubt, only some but not all of these true extensional correlations would ever be seriously supposed to be instances of natural laws.

From an extensional perspective, this circumstance poses a delicate predicament, since the separation of correlation descriptions that are true and laws from those that are true but not seems to presuppose some nonextensional principle of selection, which undermines the integrity of this approach. Some have thus imagined that this difference is either a 'question of context' or a 'matter of attitude'. But their concrete proposals have not been especially reassuring, since attitudinal advocates incline toward the criterion that true extensional correlations are laws when they are regarded as being laws, as if that should explain why those claims are properly regarded as laws; while the contextual advocates recommend the standard that those are laws that can be derived from scientific theories, as if theories were not sets of laws themselves.

In order to preserve an extensional approach, in other words, serious thinkers have felt compelled to appeal to blatantly circular maneuvers or to overtly question-begging strategems. Within an intensional framework, by comparsion, things are not so desperate, for there appear to be ample resources for contending with these differences without resorting to *ad hoc* principles. Even if one percent of all things-that-are-wood are things-that-are-cuckoo-clocks or ninety-nine percent of all things that-are-cuckoo-clocks are things-that-are-wood, those extensional correlations, as true descriptions of the world's history, would not therefore qualify as laws of nature. For there are processes and procedures, such as the production of plastic cuckoo-clocks, of metal cuckoo-clocks, or the passage of legislation prohibiting the use of wood in their construction, by virtue of which, in principle, these correlations could be changed— even if such things never in fact happen!

In the case of gold and of polonium[218], by contrast, matters are quite different, for there appear to be no processes or procedures, natural or contrived, by means of which the melting point of 1064°C and the half-life of 3.05 minutes could be taken away from things of those kinds—were we ever disposed to try. The intensional conception of natural laws thus displays a sense in which laws of nature are correctly viewed as negative existential propositions, which deny the existence of certain possibilities, not as logical impossibilities but rather as physical impossibilites. For laws hold as intensional relations between a reference property R, let us say, and some attribute property A, where a lawful connection obtains between those properties just in case there is no process or procedure, natural or contrived, by means of which something possessing R could lose A without also losing R, even though A is not a part of the definition of R, in language L. These are therefore *permanent properties* (Fetzer 1981, 1993).

Because the possession of A is not part of the definition of R, the possession of A by something that is R is said to be logically contingent. When A is a permanent property of R, therefore, then a corresponding subjunctive conditional (asserting what would be the case, if something were the case, whether or not it is) must be true. As a consequence, the logical form of lawlike sentences—of sentences that are laws if they are true—is that of logically contingent and unrestrictedly general subjunctive conditionals whose truth follows, necessarily, from the truth of these permanent property relations, whether they have any instances or not. Employing the symbol, '. . . ==> ___', as the subjunctive conditional, the logical form of (simple) lawlike sentences takes the following form:

**(SL) $(x)(t)(\mathbf{R}xt ==> \mathbf{A}xt)$**

which asserts that, if something $x$ were R at time $t$, then $x$ would also be A at $t$.

The attributes of (merely) extensional correlations are not properties that no members of their reference classes could be without: things-that-are-round might or might not be things-that-are-red, things-that-are-wood might or might not be things-that-are-cuckoo-clocks, and so on. As a result, these properties A are appropriately entertained as transient attributes of the members of their corresponding reference classes R. Moreover, natural laws invariably qualify as distributive rather than as collective generalizations in the sense that they attribute permanent properties A (of having a melting point of

1064°C or a half-life of 3.05 minutes) to every thing possessing the reference property R instead of summarizing the relative frequency with which those attributes occur in those populations. Thus, if attribute A is not possessed by every thing that is R, then the corresponding generalization cannot be a law.

That attribute A occurs in constant conjunction with reference property R, of course, thus constitutes a necessary but not sufficient condition for a lawful connection to obtain between them, because A might happen to be a transient property possessed by every member of a reference class R in common (such as would be the case when every cuckoo-clock is made of wood). The distributive character of natural laws stands in sharp contrast with means and modes and medians as the following columns of predicates are meant to exemplify:

**Table 7.2**  Means, Modes, and Medians

| R | A |
|---|---|
| gifted children | 130 median I.Q. |
| white Anglo-Saxons | usually Protestant |
| BMWs | average $35,000 |
| New College students | mean 600 SATs |

Even if gifted children (identified by their verbal abilities) happen to have a median IQ of 130, that attribute could not possibly be a permanent property of the members of that reference class—unless every gifted child happened to have that same IQ in common; even if white Anglo-Saxons usually are Protestants, that attribute could not possibly be a permanent property of the members of that reference class— unless every white Anglo-Saxon happened to be a Protestant; and so on. For permanent properties are properties that no member of a reference class could be without and therefore allow of no exceptions.

The apparent tension between the aims of science and the global features of its methods alluded to above thus emerges clearly from this point of view. For science aims at the discovery of natural laws on the basis of experiential findings and the inferences they sustain, yet there are no obvious 'principles of inference' relative to which any logically contingent, unrestrictedly general subjunctive conditionals *h* attributing permanent properties A to every member of suitably specified reference classes R could be established on the basis of (even quite large) finite sets of logically consistent singular sentences *e*. (If such a set were not logically consistent, then every conclusion would follow on the basis of elementary deduction; so these sets need to be logically consistent.)

The difficulties involved here are not (merely) those of warranting inferences from finite samples to infinite populations but those of warranting inferences from evidence describing (segments of) the world's actual history to hypotheses concerning the possible histories it could display, under differing initial conditions! For the logical force of natural laws as negative existential propositions not only entails that it is not the case that anything satisfies the corresponding description 'R & ~A' during the world's history (an 'ordinary' inference) but also that it is not the case that anything could satisfy those descriptions during any such history, even though such an outcome remains logically possible in relation to the language L (an 'extraordinary' inference, indeed!).

Physical properties of objects in the world—from melting points to IQs—are tendencies to display certain outcome responses under suitable conditions, which are amenable to varying degrees of strength. Things that have a melting point of 1064°C, for example, would melt if their temperature were raised to that point, but otherwise would remain solid; things with a boiling point of 3080°C would boil if their temperature were raised up to that point, but otherwise would remain liquid; and so forth. And similarly for shapes, sizes, colors, and other properties, such as half-lifes and IQs. Formalizing these properties requires introducing causal conditionals that are stronger than subjunctives.

Employing the symbol '. . . =u=> _____' as a causal conditional of universal strength u permits formal definitions of A attributes by relating relevant test conditions C1, C2, . . . , Cn, and their outcome effects, E1, E2, . . . , En, as follows:

$$\textbf{(DF) } \mathbf{A}xt =_{df} (\mathbf{C}1xt =\text{u}=> \mathbf{E}1xt^*) \ \& \ldots \& \ (\mathbf{C}nxt =\text{u}=> \mathbf{E}nxt^*);$$

for as many different test conditions and outcome responses as may occur, where $t^*$ is equal to or later than $t$ by some specific temporal interval delta. In the case of the melting point of 1064°C, therefore, it could be defined by instantiating this definitional scheme with appropriate tests and outcomes, where heating $x$ to a temperature T greater than 1064°C at would invariably (with strength $u$) bring about its melting M at $t^*$, for each such manifestation. Thus, when definitions of their attributes are conjoined with lawlike sentences of simple form, the result is a set of lawlike sentences of causal forms:

**(CL-1)** $(x)(t)[\mathbf{R}xt ==> (\mathbf{C}1xt =u=> \mathbf{E}1xt^*)]$; &

$$\ldots\ldots \&$$

**(CL-*n*)** $(x)(t)[\mathbf{R}xt ==> (\mathbf{C}nxt =u=> \mathbf{E}nxt^*)]$;

which means that every lawlike sentence of simple form is logically equivalent to a (possibly infinite) set of lawlike sentences of causal form. When being gold AU is the reference property and a melting point of 1064°C is the attribute, for example, then heating $x$ to a temperature T greater than 1064°C at would invariably (with universal strength) $u$ bring about $x$'s melting M at $t^*$, and so forth.

## 7.2  *What Is Science?*

These considerations are important ontologically, first, because correlations that do not reflect laws occur when properties are statistically related but are not nomically connected, and, second, because some test conditions and outcome responses are related probabilistically rather than deterministically. In the case of merely accidental correlations, attributes occur with specific relative frequencies in relation to reference properties, but these relations are not nomological. Formally, they reflect mere conjunctions of properties rather than subjunctive connections. And half-lives as properties of radioactive isotopes, for example, have test conditions (such as time trials) that are related to more than one outcome response (decay and non-decay, for example) by means of causal connections of merely probabilistic strength.

They are important epistemically, first, because testing a lawlike hypothesis relating an attribute A to a reference property R generally requires ascertaining when A is present or absent on the basis of its causal manifestations and, second, because attributes A1, A2, ... that are nomically related to reference properties R1, R2, ... cannot be separated from them. Conducting empirical tests of lawlike sentences of simple forms, in other words, can only be done on the basis of understanding their causal consequences, which represent (part or all of) their meaning. And establishing that a lawlike relation obtains between specific attributes and specific reference properties can only be done by attempting to violate them. If they are nomically related, it must be physically impossible for those reference properties to occur without those attributes, precisely because those attributes are permanent properties. Accounts of science that fail to incorporate Popper's conception of conjectures and attempted refutations are therefore very unlikely to succeed (Popper 1968).

In order to appreciate the inherent limitations with respect to the certainty of scientific knowledge thereby generated, let us consider three alternative conceptions of 'principles of inference' that potentially might serve to 'bridge the chasm' between evidence and hypothesis. According to these views, science is a process that proceeds in several stages more or less along the following lines:

**Table 7.3** Alternative Conceptions of Scientific Procedure

| INDUCTIVISM | DEDUCTIVISM | ABDUCTIVISM |
| --- | --- | --- |
| Observation | Conjecture | Puzzlement |
| Classification | Deduction | Speculation |
| Generalization | Experimentation | Adaptation |
| Prediction | Elimination | Explanation |

These are not the only possibilities, of course, since other views, including 'The Bayesian Way' with its infinite contours, have vocal advocates, too (Fetzer 1981; 1993); but as non-exhaustive illustrations, perhaps these three will do. Inductivism, Deductivism, and Abductivism have all been historically important and philosophically influential theoretical formulations that surely deserve serious consideration as significant alternative conceptions of scientific procedure.

Whether or not approaches of any of these kinds should or should not be taken seriously, furthermore, depends far less upon their specific details than on the sort of 'principles of inference' they propose to attain the object of inquiry. From this point of view, therefore, the Inductivist conception of scientific procedure as pattern of Observation, Classification, Generalization, and Prediction assumes importance only in relation to the basic principle of inference that establishes its foundation; thus, according to one such approach, the aim of science should be pursued by the method known as Enumerative Induction as follows:

**(EI) From '$m/n$ observed Rs are As', infer (inductively) '$m/n$ Rs are As',**

provided that a large number of Rs have been observed over a wide variety of conditions, where such inferences are subject to revision with the accumulation of additional evidence as the 'total evidence' condition requires (Salmon 1967).

If natural laws are subjunctively conditional, while relative frequencies are extensional distributions, however, then methods of this kind afford no criteria for the differentiation of those descriptions that are true-and-laws from those that are true-but-not. Even a wide variety requirement does not help: a large number of cuckoo-clocks have been observed in many different locations and at many different times under quite diverse circumstances, yet the corresponding distribution establishes no law. The pattern of Observation, Classification, and Generalization by this method thus appears incapable of satisfying conditions required for discovering laws. Moreover, its basic principle applies only to properties that are observable, excluding non-observable properties entirely.

The Deductivist conception of scientific procedure promises to do better, albeit in a negative direction, for the pattern of Conjecture, Derivation, Experimentation, and Elimination at least provides for empirical tests of genuinely lawlike claims through the employment of the deductive rule Modus Tollens as follows:

**(MT)  From 'hypothesis *h* entails *e*' and 'not-*e*', infer (deductively) 'not-*h*',**

provided that rejection is not mistaken for disproof, since the evidence upon which such inferences are based may itself turn out have been at fault, as a function of background assumptions, auxiliary hypotheses, and other sources of potential error. Because natural laws as subjunctive generalizations entail corresponding extensional distributions in the form of constant conjunctions, the discovery of even one R that is not an A is sufficient to sustain the rejection of the corresponding lawlike hypothesis, which is a non-trivial benefit.

Yet so long as explanations are arguments with premises including laws, their assertion as adequate entails their acceptance as true: insofar as laws are necessary for adequate explanations, science cannot succeed without procedures for acceptance as well as principles of rejection. The Deductivist conception nevertheless signals an enormous improvement over the Inductivist counterpart, since it encourages attempts to arrange this world's history such that it should include sets of events of evidential relevance for testing alternative hypotheses and scientific theories. It thus becomes apparent that attaining the aim of science requires recognizing the difference between confirming extensional distributions and testing lawlike claims; for the evidence relevant to lawlike claims consists of repeated attempts to refute them (Popper 1968).

The Abductivist conception thus affords an appropriate complement to the Deductivist conception, at least so long as its stages of Puzzlement, Speculation, Adaptation, and Explanation are entertained within the framework of Inference to the Best Explanation, which may be represented by the following conditions:

(IBE)  **The alternative $h$ that provides the best explanation for the available evidence $e$ is the preferable hypothesis; and when the available evidence $e$ is sufficient, the preferable hypothesis $h$ is acceptable. Thus, under those conditions, infer (inductively) that $h$ is true.**

Thus, the implementation of this standard, which presumes a likelihood measure of evidential support, assumes the specification of a set of alternative hypotheses $h1$, $h2$, . . . , $hn$, and a set of evidence sentences $e$, where hypotheses that have a higher degree of evidential support in relation to $e$ are preferable to those of a lesser degree of evidential support in relation to $e$, when $e$ includes all of the available evidence. Then, when the available evidence happens to be sufficient in quantity and quality to support an inference, the hypothesis—or hypotheses—that are preferable are also acceptable, where the addition of new hypotheses or the discovery of new evidence may significantly change the inferential situation.

**Figure 7.1**  Inference to the Best Explanation

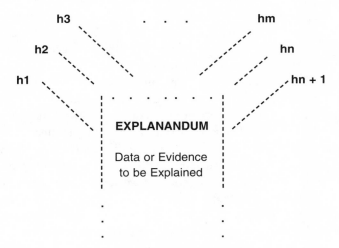

Hypotheses may be false even when they are acceptable, but they are still the most rational among the set of alternatives (Fetzer and Almeder 1993, p. 1). The likelihood measure of evidential support implements the following concept:

(LM)  From 'the nomic expectability of *e*, given *h*, equals *r*', infer (deductively) 'the measure of evidential support for *h*, given *e*, equals *r*',

where the nomic expectability of evidence e equals the logical probability for its truth, given the truth of hypothesis *h*, which must include at least one law essential to establishing the value of *r*, a matter we shall pursue. Such principles reflect likelihoods because the likelihood of hypothesis *h*, given evidence *e*, is equal to the probability of *e* on the assumption *h* is true (Fetzer 1981; 1993).

The Abductivist conception is not without its own distinctive difficulties, insofar as every consistent theory entailing an hypothesis *h* satisfying the specified conditions receives a corresponding measure of evidential support from *e*, a problem partially offset by employing explanatory relevance and irrelevance relations as a foundation for determining evidential relevance and irrelevance relations, as we are about to discover. Not the least of the problems that have been left unmentioned, however, is the need for nature's co-operation in the pursuit of scientific knowledge of natural laws; for when there are no samples at all, or only small samples, or even large but skewed samples, the available evidence may warrant either a faulty inference or no inference at all (Fetzer 1983).

This difficulty becomes acute with respect to probabilistic properties, insofar as any relative frequency within a finite sequence is logically compatible with any probabilistic attribute, even though deviations from generating probabilities become increasingly improbable as the length of such a trial sequence increases without bound. Since an atom of polonium$^{218}$ has a half-life of 3.05 minutes, its probability of undergoing decay during any 3.05 minute interval equals 1/2; but it may indefinitely remain intact, nevertheless. And although approximately half of the members of a collection of atoms of this kind would be expected to experience decay during a similar temporal interval, that might or might not occur. Thus, even over infinite sequences, it remains not merely logically but physically possible that relative frequencies may deviate from their generating probabilities.

From an epistemic point of view, perhaps the most intriguing consequence consists of the result that a physical world whose composition includes at least some probabilistic properties might be historically indistinguishable from a world whose composition includes no probabilistic properties at all—either because there are no appropriate trials, or too few appropriate trials, or enough appropriate trials that, by chance, happen to yield unrepresentative frequencies. So even if a world were indeterministic in its character (by instantiating probabilistic as well as non-probabilistic properties), the history of that world might turn out to be indistinguishable from the history of a deterministic world insofar as they might both display exactly the same relative frequencies and constant conjunctions, where their differences were concealed 'by chance'!

Thus, if some of the world's properties are probabilistic, not only may the same laws generate different world-histories, but the same world-histories may be generated by different laws—under identical initial conditions! Indeed, the most important implication attending these considerations deserves explicit recognition, since even if our available evidence could describe the world's entire history, fundamental aspects of its physical structure, including the deterministic or indeterministic character of its laws, might remain undiscovered, nevertheless. The tension between the aim of science and the global features of its methods is therefore inherent and cannot be overcome: the uncertainty of scientific knowledge is an unavoidable consequence of the nature of natural laws.

## 7.3 Is Creationism Science?

As we have found, the debate over whether creationism should be taught in the public-school science curriculum depends upon at least two crucial factors: the nature of creationism and the nature of science. The significance of our exploration of the nature of science may be evaluated by its application to three classic creationist hypotheses, which deserve consideration within this context. Each assumes that God is the creator of the universe and asserts, respectively:

(CC-1)  **God created the world and everything therein exactly as it is today;**

(CC-2)  **God created the world and everything therein, including life in fixed and unchanging forms; and,**

(CC-3)  **God created the world and everything therein, including all forms of life by means of evolution.**

These classic hypotheses do not exhaust Creationist alternatives, especially its contemporary Creation Science guise, and I considered those
kinds of Creationist hypotheses in Chapter 1. When we attempt to
appraise their scientific standing on the basis of the three conceptions of
science, however, they do not appear to yield the same results. This process
therefore serves not only as a test of the scientific standing of these
Creationist hypotheses but also of the success of our analysis of science.

Consider, for example, the difference between the results of
Inductivist and Deductivist appraisals of (CC-2). Inductivism, of course,
adopts (EI) as the basic principle of scientific inference, according to
which, if $m/n$ observed Rs are As, infer (inductively) $m/n$ Rs are As. The
hypothesis that God created the world and everything therein, including
life in fixed and unchanging forms, could presumably be inferred by
means of this principle if it were possible (a) to observe n living things as
instances of R and (b) to ascertain the proportion $m/n$ of them that were
created by God in forms that are fixed and unchanging as instances of A.
(When every instances of R is an instance of A, of course, then $m/n = 1$.)
The evident problem encountered here is not observing living things but
observing which among them were created by God in forms that are fixed
and unchanging.

The problem is less that of observing forms of life that are fixed and
unchanging than that of observing that God created them. The conclusion that (CC-2) cannot qualify as a scientific hypothesis on Inductivist
standards thus appears to be a consequence of the restriction of (EI)
exclusively to observable properties. Deductivism, by contrast, adopts
(MT) as the basic principle of scientific inference, according to which,
from 'hypothesis $h$ entails $e$' and 'not-$e$', infer (deductively) 'not-$h$'. If
(CC-2) entails that (all) living things were created in forms that are fixed
and unchanging, that implies in turn that (all) living things exist in forms
that are fixed and unchanging, which would appear to be something that,
under suitable conditions, could be subject to empirical test. The issue
is not the truth of (CC-2), but whether, according to (MT) standards,
(CC-2) qualifies as scientific.

Thus, if it were possible to discover even one species (such as bacteria,
for example) that does not exist in forms that are fixed and unchanging,
then hypothesis (CC-2) could be rejected as false—inconclusively, of
course, since the discovery of new evidence, such as that old evidence was
acquired on the basis of background assumptions or auxiliary hypotheses
that turn out to have been in error or wrong, could undermine previous
findings and require their revision. Thus, it should be apparent that the
employment of deductive priciples within scientific contexts is a form of

conclusive reasoning where conclusions that are derived on the basis of those principles cannot be false—provided the premises upon which they are based are true! The crucial point with regard to (CC-2), however, is not that the application of (MT) in empirical contexts is fallible but that (CC-2) appears to be testable.

That Inductivist and Deductivist appraisals of creationist hypotheses, such as (CC-2), might support conflicting conclusions is a striking result. The conclusion that hypothesis (CC-2) is unscientific relative to (EI), however, might be altered by reducing (CC-2) strictly to the claim that the properties of species are fixed and do not change. The determination that the creationist hypothesis qualifies as 'scientific' when the role of God is disregarded, however, would be a Pyrrhic victory for creationism, since the role of God is indispensable to it. It is therefore all the more fascinating that, when the role of God is appropriately retained, Inductism and Deductivism yield conflicting evaluations, where (CC-2) apparently qualifies as 'scientific' in relation to (MT) but not in relation to (EI).

The question is not reducible to one of truth or falsity. No doubt, the Creationist hypothesis may turn out to be false insofar as it implies that the properties of species are fixed and do not change, because the available evidence might not support that conclusion. Nevertheless, that would not be enough to show that creationism is unscientific. Classical Newtonian mechanics, for example, has been superseded by Einsteinian relativity and is no longer held to be true, but that has not altered its standing as a scientific theory. Nevertheless, the standards imposed by Inductivism and Deductivism cannot qualify as definitive, since Abductivism appears to provide a far more adequate conception of the nature of science. The question thus becomes that of whether creationist hypotheses such as (CC-2) are scientific by its standards.

According to Abductivism, the basic priciple of inference is (IBE), according to which, from 'the nomic expectability of *e*, given *h*, equals *r*', infer (deductively) 'the measure of evidential support for *h*, given *e*, equals *r*'. We have found that there are two aspects to the application of this principle, namely: that a hypothesis would be preferable to another when it provides a better explanation of the available evidence than does the other; and that the preferable hypothesis would be acceptable when enough evidence happens to be available. In criminal cases, this distinction corresponds to the difference between having a suspect in a crime and having enough evidence for an arrest. Someone can be the strongest suspect ('preferable') relative to the evidence available without the available evidence being sufficient to indict or to convict him ('acceptable').

What's most interesting about the application of (IBE) to creationism is that it properly applies to sets of alternative hypotheses, where each member of this set qualifies as an alternative explanation of the available evidence. In order to qualify as an 'alternative explanation', however, a hypothesis has to advance a 'possible explanation' for the available evidence, that is, it must qualify as an explanation that would be adequate if it were true. The question with which we are concerned, therefore, is not whether creationist hypotheses (CC-1) to (CC-3) are true, but whether each qualifies as a possible explanation for the evidence *e*, which includes the fossil record, geological strata, morphological similarities, and so forth.

**Figure 7.2** Are Creationist Hypotheses Scientific?

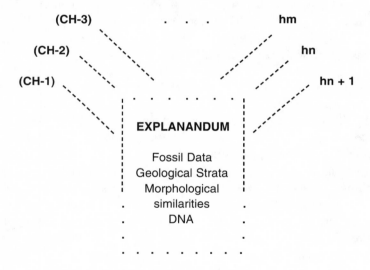

The conditions that must be satisfied for a hypothesis *h* to qualify as a possible explanation for evidence e are commonly specified by entertaining explanations as arguments, where the premises are known as the *explanans* and the conclusion as the *explanandum*. Strictly speaking, a distinction must be drawn between the 'explanandum-phenomenon' as a feature of the physical world and the 'explanandum-sentence' as a description of some particular aspect of the phenomenon for which an explanation is desired. The explanandum-phenomenon is then explained by subsuming that phenomenon within the scope of a 'covering law', which might be deterministic or probabilistic, which may be accomplished linguistically by deriving—deductively or probabilistically—the explanandum as conclusion from the explanans as its premises.

Then the occurrence of the phenomenon described by an explanandum-sentence has an adequate scientific explanation in the form of its corresponding explanans when it satisfies the following four conditions of adequacy, namely:

(CA-1)   **the explanandum can be derived—deductively or probabilistically—as a (deductive or probabilisitic) consequence from its explanans;**

(CA-2)   **the explanans contains at least one lawlike sentence (a sentence that would be a law if it were true)—of either universal or probabilistic form—that is required for the derivation specified by (CA-1);**

(CA-3)   **the explanans must exclude irrelevant properties that make no difference to the occurrence of the explanandum, a condition that is now known as the requirement of strict maximal specificity; and,**

(CA-4)   **the sentences that constitute the explanation—both the explanans and the explanandum—must be true. (Fetzer 1981, 1993)**

This conception supports the conclusion that there are at least two different kinds of explanation, one of which invokes a deterministic law and supports the deductive derivation of its explanandum, the other of which invokes a probabilistic law and supports the inductive derivation of its explanandum, which can be called 'deterministic-deductive' and 'probabilistic-inductive'.

A simple example of a deterministic-deductive explanation could explain why a match made of a specific chemical composition lights when it is struck in a particular way, when the match is dry and oxygen is present, as follows:

**Figure 7.3** A Deterministic-Deductive Explanation

| | | |
|---|---|---|
| Law: | Striking a match of kind K under condition $C_i$ would cause it to light. | |
| | | EXPLANANS |
| Initial Conditions: | This is a match of kind K being struck under conditions $C_i$ now. | |
| | —————————————— | |
| Description of Event: | This match is lighting now. | EXPLANANDUM |

In order for its lawlike premise to be true, the antecedent of that sentence (its 'if' clause) has to specify the presence or the absence of every property whose presence or absence makes a difference to the occurrence of its consequent (its 'then' claus), a condition that is known as *the requirement of maximal specificity*. Suppose, for example, that the presence or absence of oxygen happened to omitted from consideration. Then that sentence would be false, because lighting would occur when oxygen was present, but otherwise not (Fetzer 1981; 1993).

As Hempel (1965) forcefully emphasized, deterministic-deductive explanations are potentially predictive, in the sense that, had their premises been taken account of at a suitable prior time, it would have been possible to predict the occurrence of the explanandum phenomenon on the basis of those premises. Probabilistic-inductive explanations, however, do not display this property, since the occurrence of an outcome that occurs with a certain fixed probability may or may not occur with high probability, say, probability $> .5$. When an outcome, such as radioactive decay, occurs with a high probability, such as .9, then its alternative, such as non-decay, must occur with low probability, such as .1. Ordinarily, however, the occurrence of an event would not be predicted unless its probability were $> .5$. The premises that could explain outcomes of low probability, therefore, do not tend to support their prediction.

It's tempting to suppose that every inference from premises including laws must be explanatory, as, indeed, Hempel was inclined to think (Hempel 1965, pp. 173–74). However, it's not difficult to discover examples that show that to be a mistaken conception. Consider inferences involving premises that concern various conditions sufficient to bring about the death of those to whom they are subject, such as being run over by a steamroller (being stepped upon by an elephant, and so on). That you and I are still alive permits a retrodictive inference from the present to the past of the following kind:

**Figure 7.4** A Retrodictive Inference

| Law: | Being run over by a steamroller would bring about your death. | |
|---|---|---|
| | | PREMISES |
| Initial Conditions: | You are not dead. | |
| | _____ | |
| Description of Event: | You have not been run over by a steamroller. | CONCLUSION |

This argument, which involves the deduction of a conclusion from premises including at least one law that is actually required for this derivation, is nevertheless non-explanatory. While it permits the inference that you have not been run over by a steamroller, it does not explain why! The explanatory failure of cases of this kind appears to be rooted in their appeal to 'initial conditions' that occur at times subsequent to the occurrence of the phenomena they are being used to retrodict (Fetzer 1992).

Perhaps even more instructive within the present context, explanations suffer from another variety of inadequacy when their explanans-premises include properties whose presence or absence makes no difference to the occurrence of the explanandum-phenomenon. Consider the following 'explanation':

**Figure 7.5**  An Inadequate Explanation

| | | |
|---|---|---|
| Law: | Men who take birth control pills do not become pregnant. | |
| | | EXPLANANS |
| Initial Conditions: | John Jones has been taking birth control pills. | |
| | _____ | |
| Description of Event: | John Jones has not become pregnant. | EXPLANANDUM |

The striking feature of this 'explanation' is that the explanandum does indeed follow from its explanans, thereby satisfying adequacy condition (CA-1), where the derivation of the explanandum from its explanans does indeed require a lawlike premise, thereby satisfying adequacy condition (CA-2). The problem is that men do not become pregnant whether they take birth control pills or not, which means this argument violates adequacy condition (CA-3).

When (IBE) is being employed as a principle of inference, of course, we don't know which among the available alternatives satisfies condition (CA-4), which is the truth condition. (If we did, we would not need inference to the best explanation to find out!) The requirements that must be satisfied for an hypothesis to be a possible explanation and thereby qualify for inclusion within a set of alternative hypotheses $h1$, $h2, \ldots, hn$ that might be preferable or even acceptable, in relation to specified explananda or available evidence $e$, therefore, are (CA-1), derivability, (CA-2), lawlikeness, and (CA-3), the exclusion of irrelevant factors. Classic creationist hypotheses, such as (CC-1), (CC-2), and (CC-3), therefore, will qualify as scientific hypotheses if and only if they can satisfy these three conditions and thereby establish that they are possible scientific explanations for *e*.

From this perspective, the problems encountered by classic creationist hypotheses become obvious. (CC-1), for example, which asserts that God created the world and everything therein exactly as it is today, cannot satisfy (CA-1). The phrase, 'exactly as it is today', after all, would describe the world no matter what its properties, including the presence or the absence of the fossil record, geological strata, morphological similarities, and the like. No descriptions of any evidence or explananda are derivable from (CC-1), which therefore cannot qualify as a possible explanation that might be adequate if it were true. As a consequence, (CC-1) cannot qualify as a scientific alternative, because it does not satisfy the condition of adequacy (CA-1) for a possible scientific explanation.

(CC-2), which asserts that God created the world and everything therein, including life in fixed and unchanging forms, by comparison, at least implies potential explananda, namely: that life exists in forms that are fixed and unchanging. To this extent, at least, therefore, (CC-2) appears to satisfy (CA-1). The problem is that the derivation of the potential explanandum—that life exists in forms that are fixed and unchanging—follows from (CC-2) without making any appeal to any laws. In particular, there are no laws that relate antecedent conditions (concerning God's disposition to create worlds and life forms, for example) that could be invoked in support of such an inference. Even assuming that God had such a disposition, (CC-2) cannot satisfy (CA-2) and therefore does not qualify as a potential scientific explanation. As a consequence, (CC-2) also cannot qualify as a scientific hypothesis.

It could be argued that the claim that life exists in forms that are fixed and unchanging has a lawlike character, since it implies that, no matter what conditions might happen to be realized during the course of the world's history, those forms could not be changed. A similar argument could be made with respect to (CC-3), which asserts that God created the world and everything therein, including all life forms by means of evolution—at least, when the assumption is made that evolution provides a suitable set of causal mechanisms to account for the phenomena. In this case, (CC-3) satisfies not only (CA-1) but (CA-2) as well. The problem is, however, that if evolution provides a set of causal mechanisms that is suitable to account for the phenomena, an appeal to God is no longer necessary. This hypothesis fails to satisfy (CA-3) and thus also fails to qualify as a scientific alternative.

From the perspective of inference to the best explanation, therefore, none of these classic creationist hypotheses qualify as scientific alternatives, since none of them qualifies as a possible explanation for the phenomena. That this should be the case, moreover, becomes especially apparent when consideration is given to (LM), which asserts that, from 'the nomic expectability of $e$, given $h$, equals $r$', infer (deductively) 'the measure of evidential support for $h$, given $e$, equals $r$'. The nomic expectability of evidence $e$ equals the logical probability of its truth, given the truth of hypothesis $h$, where the value of $r$ may be measured by the extent to which the explanandum phenomenon would be expected (or could be derived) from an explanans that includes at least one essential law. When the explanans contains no essential law, the nomic expectability of $e$, given $h$, is 0.

That the half-life of polonium[218] is 3.05 minutes not only means that a single atom has a probability of 1/2 to decay during a 3.05 minute interval but also implies that that same atom has a probability of 1/2 to not undergo decay during that same interval. It also implies that, for large numbers of atoms of polonium[218] given at a specific time, very close to one-half will still exist 3.05 minutes later, the remainder having disintegrated by decay (Hempel 1966, p. 66). If the half-life of polonium[218] were not known, repeated observations of decay on this order would support such an inference as the hypothesis that provides the best explanation for the frequency data. This would be the hypothesis with the highest likelihood, given the evidence.

Alternative hypotheses that might deserve consideration would include those that cluster around the observed relative frequency of decay in large samples, which would have values close to 3.05 minutes. Those hypotheses would have high likelihoods by virtue of making those outcomes highly probable, which indicates that more than one hypothesis can have high likelihood (Fetzer 1981, p. 276). When repeated sequences of trials are conducted under suitable test conditions and yield stable relative frequencies for decay, the hypothesis with the highest likelihood would deserve to be accepted. Indeed, the convergence of statistical data toward a normal distribution affords a measure that supports the presumption those trials were random and can be employed to determine when the available evidence is suffcient (Fetzer 1981, Chapter 9). The distribution of the data thus sustains inferences about its evidential value.

When the nomic expectability of $e$, given $h$, is 0, of course, the measure of evidential support for $h$, given $e$, is also 0. It should come as no surprise, therefore, that creationist hypotheses, such as (CC-1) and (CC-2), that confer no nomic expectability upon the explanandum, cannot have measures of evidential support greater than 0. Moreover, if (CC-2) and (CC-3) are defended on the ground that the existence of life in forms that are fixed and unchanging or the creation of life by means of evolution possess lawlike standing, it should be evident that their lawlike standing does not depend upon invoking God as the creator, which means that whatever explanatory potential they may possess does not depend upon God, which makes God irrelevant and thus defeats the creationist program. Even if classic creationist hypotheses are not scientific, however, that does not show that evolution is scientific or that other alternatives cannot do better.

When (IBE) is used to draw inferences concerning the occurrence of specific phenomena, such as singular events $e$, alternative explanations, $hi$, may include both lawlike generalizations and initial conditions. When (IBE) is used to draw inferences concerning lawlike generalizations, e may include relative frequencies for specific outcomes in relation to initial conditions. Either way, evidence $e$ supports hypothesis $h1$ better than hypothesis $h2$ when the likelihood of $h1$, given $e$, exceeds that of $h2$, or when the likelihood ratio of $h1$, given $e$, to $h2$, exceeds 1 (Hacking 1965). If $h1$ were an evolutionary hypothesis and $h2$ a creationist hypothesis, then even if the likelihood of $h1$ given e were very low—because the nomic expectability for evidence $e$, given $h1$, was very low—$h1$ nevertheless could be highly preferable to $h2$ given $e$—because the nomic expectability for $e$, given $h2$, was 0. So even if the nomic expectability for evidence $e$, given evolution, should turn out to be very low, it could still be not only a preferable alternative but even an acceptable one.

The debate over whether Creationism ought to be taught as part of the science curriculum in pubic schools cannot be intelligently discussed, much less resolved, without justifiable conceptions of the nature of science, on the one hand, and of the nature of Creationism, on the other. By exploring three of the most influential models of science—Inductivism, Deductivism, and Abductivism—a foundation has been laid for addressing these and related issues, including the scientific standing of evolutionary theory. Those who persist in holding that classic Creationist hypotheses are scientific incur an intellectual obligation to identify and justify the conception of science that would yield a more favorable outcome for Creationism than has been established here.

# References

Angier, N. 1997. Survey of Scientists Finds a Stability of Faith in God. *New York Times* (3rd April), p. A10.

Applebome, P. 1996. For Pope, Faith and Science Coexist. *New York Times* (25th October), p. A4.

Arnold, A.J., and K. Fristrup. 1982, The Theory of Evolution by Natural Selection: A Hierarchical Expansion, *Paleobiology* 8 (1982), pp. 113–129.

Asimov, I. 1987. *Beginning: The Story of Origins—Of Mankind, Life, the Earth, the Universe*. New York: Berkely, 1987.

Associated Press. 2005. Federal Judge Rules Against 'Intelligent Design'. azcentral.com (20th December).

Bear, M.F., *et al.* 2001. *Neuroscience: Exploring the Brain*. Second edition (Baltimore: Lippincott, Williams, and Wilkins).

Beatty, J. and S. Feinsen. 1989. Rethinking the Propensity Interpretation: A Peek Inside Pandora's Box. In M. Ruse, ed., *What the Philosophy of Biology Is: Essays for David Hull* (Dordrecht: Kluwer), pp. 17–31.

Behe, M. 1996. *Darwin's Black Box: The Biochemical Challenge to Evolution* (New York: The Free Press).

Berra, T.M. 1990. *Evolution and the Myth of Creationism*. Stanford: Stanford University Press.

Boas, R. 1960. *A Primer of Real Functions*. New York: Wiley.

Bonner, J.T. 1980, *The Evolution of Culture in Animals*. Princeton: Princeton University Press.

———. 1988. *The Evolution of Complexity by Means of Natural Selection*. Princeton: Princeton University Press.

Boyd, R. 1997. Set on a Path Before Birth. *Duluth News-Tribune* (14th March), pp. 1A, 4A.

Brandon, R. 1982. The Levels of Selection. In P. Asquith and T. Nickles, eds., *PSA 1982*, Volume 1 (East Lansing: Philosophy of Science Association), pp. 315–322.

Brandon, R., and R. Burian, eds. 1984. *Genes, Populations, Organisms: Controversies over the Units of Selection* (Cambridge, Massachusetts: MIT Press).

Brandon, R.N., and S. Carson. 1996. The Indeterministic Character of Evolutionary Theory: No 'No Hidden Variable Proof' but No Room for Determinism Either. *Philosophy of Science* 63, pp. 315–337.

Broder, J. 1997. Cigarette Maker Concedes Smoking Can Cause Cancer. *New York Times* (21st March), pp. A1, A12.

Brown, W. 1995, *In the Beginning: Compelling Evidence for Creation and the Flood*, Special Edition. Phoenix: Center for Creation Science.

Clifford, W.K. 1879, The Ethics of Belief. In W.K. Clifford, *Lectures and Essays*, Volume II (London: Macmillan), pp. 177–211.

Cosmides, L. 1985. Deduction or Darwinian Algorithms? An Explanation of the 'Elusive' Content Effect on the Wason Selection Task. Cambridge, Massachusetts: Ph.D. Dissertation, Harvard University.

———. 1989. The Logic of Social Exchange: Has Natural Selection Shaped How Humans Reason? Studies with the Wason Selection Task, *Cognition* 31, pp. 187–276.

Cosmides, L., and J. Tooby. 1987. From Evolution to Behavior: Evolutionary Psychology as the Missing Link. In J. Dupre, ed., *The Latest on the Best: Essays on Evolution and Optimality* (Cambridge, Massachusetts: MIT Press), pp. 277–306.

Davies, P. 1983. *God and the New Physics*. New York: Simon and Schuster.

Davies, P.S., J. H. Fetzer, and T. Foster. 1995. Logical Reasoning and Domain Specificity: A Critique of the Social Exchange Theory of Reasoning. *Biology and Philosophy* 10, pp. 1–37.

Davis, Percival, and Dean H. Kenyon. 1989/1993. *Of Pandas and People: The Central Question of Biological Origins*. Second edition. Richardson: Foundation for Thought and Ethics.

Dawkins, R. 1986. *The Blind Watchmaker: Why the Evidence of Evolution Reveals a Universe without Design*. New York: Norton.

Deacon, T. 1997, *The Symbolic Species*. London: Allen Lane.

Dennett, D. 1995. *Darwin's Dangerous Idea: Evolution and the Meanings of Life*. New York: Simon and Schuster.

Dupre, J. ed., 1987. *The Latest on the Best*. Cambridge, Massachusetts: MIT Press.

Ehrman, Brad. 2005. *Misquoting Jesus: The Story Behind Who Changed the Bible and Why*. San Francisco: HarperSanFrancisco.

Escchenmoser, A. 1999. Chemical Etiology of Nucleic Acid Struture. *Science* 284 (15th June), pp. 2088–2124.

Ferguson, K. 1991. *Stephen Hawking: Quest for a Theory of Everything*. New York: Bantam.

Fetzer, J.H. 1981. *Scientific Knowledge: Causation, Explanation, and Corroboration*. Dordrecht: Reidel.

———. 1983. Transcendent Laws and Empirical Procedures. In N. Rescher, ed., *The Limits of Lawfulness* (Lanham: University Press of America), pp. 25–32.

————. 1988a. Probabilistic Metaphysics. In J. Fetzer ed., *Probability and Causality* (Dordrecht: Reidel), pp. 109–132.

————. 1990. *Artificial Intelligence: Its Scope and Limits.* Dordrecht: Kluwer.

————. 1991a. Thesis: Evolution Is Not an Optimizing Process. Human Behavior and Evolution Society-List HBES-L Internet (6th November).

————. 1991b. Survival of the Fittest: A Response to Eric Smith and Kim Hill. Human Behavior and Evolution Society-List HBES-L Internet (12th November).

————. 1991c. Probabilities and Frequencies in Evolutionary Theory: Response to the Replies of Eric Smith and Kim Hill. Human Behavior and Evolution Society-List HBES-L Internet (19th November).

————. 1991/96. *Philosophy and Cognitive Science,* second edition. St. Paul: Paragon.

————. 1992. What's Wrong with Salmon's History: The Fourth Decade. *Philosophy of Science* 59, pp. 246–262.

————. 1993. *Philosophy of Science.* New York: Paragon.

————. 1994. Mental Algorithms: Are Minds Computational Systems? *Pragmatics and Cognition* 2, pp. 1–29.

————. 1996. *Philosophy and Cognitive Science,* second edition. St. Paul: Paragon.

————. 1997. Intelligence vs. Mentality: Important but Independent Concepts. In A. Meystel, ed., *Proceedings of the 1997 International Conference on Intelligent Systems and Semiotics* (Gaithersburg: National Institute of Standards and Technology), pp. 493–498.

————. 1998. People Are Not Computers: Most Thought Processes are Not Computational Procedures. *Journal of Theoretical and Experimental AI* 10, pp. 371–391.

————. 2001. *Computers and Cognition: Why Minds Are Not Machines.* Dordrecht: Kluwer.

————. 2002. Evolving Consciousness: The Very Idea! *Evolution and Cognition* 8:2, pp. 230–240;

————. 2004. The Ethics of Belief: Taking Religion out of Public Policy Debates, *Bridges* 11:3–4, pp. 247–278.

————. 2005. *The Evolution of Intelligence: Are Humans the Only Animals with Minds?* Chicago: Open Court.

Fetzer, J.H., and R. Almeder. 1993. *Glossary of Epistemology/Philosophy of Science.* New York: Paragon.

Feynman, R., R. Leighton, and M. Sands. 1963, *The Feynman Lectures in Physics,* Volume 1. Reading, Massachusetts: Addison-Wesley.

Forey, P. 1988. *An Instant Guide to Dinosaurs and Prehistoric Life.* Stamford: Longmeadow.

Gamow, G. 1954. Modern Cosmology. *Scientific American* 190 (March), pp. 55–63.

Garrett, L. 1995, *The Coming Plague.* New York: Penguin.

Gerard, G. 2006. Gene Gerard: Religion Running Roughshod Over Cancer Science. www.truthdig.com/report/print/20060611_gene_gerard_religion_cancer_science.

Ghiselin, M. 1997. *Metaphysics and the Origin of Species*. Albany: State University of New York Press.

Glymour, C. 1998. What Went Wrong? Reflections on Science by Observation and *The Bell Curve*. *Philosophy of Science* 65, pp. 1–32.

Goldberg, C. 1999. On Web, Models Auction Their Eggs to Bidders for Beautiful Children. *New York Times* (23rd October), p. A10.

Goodstein, L. 2005. Judge Glad to Tackle Intelligent-Design Case. *Duluth News Tribune* (18th December), p. 5A.

Gould, J., and C. Gould. 1996. *Sexual Selection: Mate Choice, and Courtship in Nature*. New York: Scientific American Library.

Grobel, L. 1999. Interview: Jesse Ventura. *Playboy* (November).

Gustason, W., and D. Ulrich. 1973. *Elementary Symbolic Logic*. New York: Holt, Rinehart.

Hacking, I. 1965. *Logic of Statististical Inference*. Cambridge: Cambridge University Press.

Harris, G. 2006. Panel Unanimously Recommends Cervical Cancer Vaccine for Girls 11 and Up. *New York Times* (30th June), p. A12.

Hawking, S. 1988. *A Brief History of Time: From the Big Bang to Black Holes*. New York: Bantam.

Hempel, Carl G. 1962. Rational Action. Reprinted in N. Care and C. Landesman, eds., *Readings in the Theory of Action* (Bloomington: Indiana University Press, 1962), pp. 281–305.

———. 1965. Science and Human Values. In C.G. Hempel, *Aspects of Scientific Explanation* (New York: Free Press, 1965), pp. 81–96.

———. 1966. *Philosophy of Natural Science*. Englewood Cliffs: Prentice Hall.

Herrnstein, R., and C. Murray. 1994. *The Bell Curve: Intelligence and Class Structure in American Life*. New York: Free Press.

Hill, K. 1991a. Re Fetzer on Optimizing vs. Satisficing, Human Behavior and Evolution Society-List HBES-L Internet (7th November).

Hill, K. 1991b. From Kim Hill, Human Behavior and Evolution. Society-List HBES-L Internet (13th November).

Hilts, P. 1996. Fierce Bacteria Strain Is a Worldwide Problem. *New York Times* (25th July), p. A6.

Hoyle, F. 1950. *The Nature of the Universe*. New York: Harper.

Hull, D. 1978. A Matter of Individuality. *Philosophy of Science* 45, pp. 335–360.

Hulse, C. 2006. Flag Amendment Narrowly Fails in Senate Vote. *New York Times* 28 (June), p. A1.

Ibn Warraq. 1995. *Why I Am Not a Muslim*. Amherst: Prometheus.

———, ed. 2000. *The Quest for the Historical Muhammad*. Amherst: Prometheus.

James, W. 1879. *The Will to Believe and Other Essays in Popular Philosophy*. London: Longmans.

Johnson, G. 1999. How Is the Universe Built? Grain by Grain. *New York Times* 7 (December), pp. F1, F6.

Johnson, T., *et al.* 1996. Late Pleistocene Desiccation of Lake Victoria and Rapid Evolution of Chiclid Fishes. *Science* 273, pp 1091–93.

Johnston, D. 1999. Gap Between Rich, Poor has Grown Wider. *Duluth News Tribune* 5 (September), p. 17A.

Jones, J.E. 2004. Memorandum Opinion: Tammy Kitzmiller, *et al.*, Plaintiffs, v. Dover Area School District, *et al.*, Defendants, Case No. 04cv2688. US District Court for the Middle District of Pennsylvannia (20th December 2005).

Kandel, E.R. *et al.* 2000. Principles of Neural Science. New York: McGraw Hill.

Kelly, M. 2001. *The Divine Right of Capital*. San Francisco: Berrett-Koehler.

Kleene, S.C. 1967. *Mathematical Logic*. New York: Wiley.

Kuhn, T.S. 1957. *The Copernican Revolution*. Cambridge, Massachusetts: Harvard University Press.

Kuhn, T.S. 1962. *The Structure of Scientific Revolutions*. Chicago: University of Chicago Press.

Lemonick, M., and A. Dorfman. 1999. Up From the Apes. *Time* 23 (August), pp. 50–58.

Lennox, J. 1992. The Philosophy of Biology. In M. Salmon *et al.*, eds., *Introduction to the Philosophy of Science* (Englewood Cliffs: Prentice Hall), pp. 269–309.

Lerner, E. 1992. *The Big Bang Never Happened*. New York: Vantage.

Lewis, R. 1995. *Life*. Second edition. Dubuque: Brown.

Lumsden, C., and E.O. Wilson. 1981. *Genes, Mind, and Culture*. Cambridge, Massachusetts: Harvard University Press.

Lumsden, C., and E.O. Wilson. 1983. *Promethean Fire: Reflections on the Origin of Mind*. Cambridge, Massachusetts: Harvard University Press.

Malinowski, B. 1960. *A Scientific Theory of Culture*. New York: Galaxy.

Margulis, L., and D. Sagan. 1986. *Origins of Sex: Three Billion Years of Genetic Recombination*. New Haven: Yale University Press.

Mayr, E. 1982. *The Growth of Biological Thought*. Cambridge, Massachusetts: Harvard University Press.

Mayr, E. 1988. *Toward a New Philosophy of Biology*. Cambridge, Massachusetts: Harvard University Press.

McGinnis, B. 2005. Intelligent Design Can Be Tested Scientifically. http://www.loveallpeople.org/intelligentdesign1.html.

McWilliams, P. 1996. *Ain't Nobody's Business if You Do: The Absurdity of Consensual Crimes in Our Free Country*. Prelude Press, Reprint edition.

Michalos, A. 1969. *Principles of Logic*. Englewood Cliffs: Prentice-Hall.

———. 1973. Rationality between the Maximizers and the Satisficers. *Policy Sciences* 4, pp. 229–244.

Michod, R. 1995. *Eros and Evolution: A Natural Philosophy of Sex*. Reading, Massachusetts: Addison–Wesley.

Mills, S., and J. Beatty. 1979. The Propensity Interpretation of Fitness. *Philosophy of Science* 46, pp. 263–286.

Morris, H. 1974. *Scientific Creationism*. General Edition. El Cajon: Master Books.

Munitz, M., ed. 1957. *Theories of the Universe*. New York: Free Press.

Murray, C. 1996. Afterword. In R. Herrnstein and C. Murray, *The Bell Curve: Intelligence and Class Structure in American Life* (New York: The Free Press), pp. 553–575.

Niiniluoto, I. 1988. Probability, Possibility, and Plenitude. In J. Fetzer, ed., *Probability and Causality* (Dordrecht: Kluwer), pp. 91–108.

Numbers, R.L. 1993. *The Creationists: The Evolution of Scientific Creationism*. Berkeley: University of California Press.

Orr, H.A. 2005. Devolution: Why Intelligent Design Isn't. *New Yorker* (30th May).

Parker, G. A., and J. Maynard Smith. 1990. Optimality Theory in Evolutionary Biology. *Nature* 348, pp. 27–33.

Popper, K.R. 1968. *Conjectures and Refutations*. New York: Harper and Row.

Quine, W.V. 1951. *Mathematical Logic*. New York: Harper and Row.

———. 1960. *Word and Object*. Cambridge, Massachusetts: MIT Press.

Rachels, J. 1999. *The Elements of Moral Philosophy*. New York: McGraw Hill.

Rachels, J. 2003. *The Right Thing to Do*. New York: McGraw-Hill.

Richards, R. 1987. *Darwin and the Emergence of Evolutionary Theories of Mind and Behavior*. Chicago: University of Chicago Press.

Richardson, R.C. 1994. Optimization in Evolutionary Ecology. In D. Hull *et al.*, eds., *PSA 1994*, Volume 1 (East Lansing: Philosophy of Science Association), pp. 13–21.

Richardson, R.C. 1998. Heuristics and Satisficing. In W. Bechtel and G. Graham, eds., *A Companion to Cognitive Science* (Malden: Blackwell), pp. 566–575.

Richardson, R.C., and R.M. Burian. 1992. A Defense of the Propensity Interpretation of Fitness. In D. Hull *et al.*, eds., *PSA 1992*, Volume 2 (East Lansing: Philosophy of Science Association), pp. 349–362.

Ridley, M. 1993. *The Red Queen: Sex and the Evolution of Human Nature*. New York: Macmillan.

Rogers, A. 1999. The Big Bang Is Back. *Newsweek* (16th August), pp. 56–57.

Rogers, E. 1960. *Physics for the Inquiring Mind*. Princeton: Princeton University Press.

Rosenhouse, J. 2006. Why Is It Unconstitutional to Teach Intelligent Design? http://www.csicop.org/intelligentdesignwatch/dover.html.

Ruse, M. 1998. *Taking Darwin Seriously*. Amherst: Prometheus, 1998.

Ruse, M., and E.O. Wilson. 1985. The Evolution of Ethics. *New Scientist* 17, pp. 50–52.

———. 1986. Moral Philosophy as Applied Science. *Philosophy* 61, pp. 173–192.

Rushton, J.P. 1996. Political Correctness and the Study of Racial Differences. *Journal of Social Distress and the Homeless* 5, pp. 213–229.

Russell, B. 1957. *Why I Am Not a Christian*. New York: Simon and Schuster.

Sadler, T.W. 1990. *Langman's Medical Embryology*. Sixth edition. Baltimore: Williams and Wilkins.

Salmon, W.C. 1967. *The Foundations of Scientific Inference.* Pittsburgh: University of Pittsburgh Press.

Schmidt, K. 1996. Creationists Evolve New Strategy. *Science* 273 (26th July), pp. 420–422.

Schuler, G.D. *et al.* 1996, A Gene Map of the Human Genome. *Science* 274 (25th October), pp. 540–546.

Scoccia, D. 1990. Utilitarianism, Sociobiology, and the Limits of Benevolence. *Journal of Philosophy* LVII, pp. 329–345.

Shermer, M. 2000. *How We Believe: The Search for God in an Age of Science.* New York: Freeman.

Smith, E. 1991a. Re Fetzer on Optimizing vs. Satisficing, Human Behavior, and Evolution. Society-List HBES-L Internet (6th November).

————. 1991b. Rebuttal to Fetzer's Reply. Human Behavior and Evolution Society-List HBES-L Internet (16th November).

Sober, E. 1984. *The Nature of Selection: Evolutionary Theory in Philosophical Perspective.* Cambridge, Massachusetts: MIT Press.

Stevens, W. 1999. Rearranging the Branches on a New Tree of Life. *New York Times* (31st August), pp. D1, D7.

Stinnett, R. 1999. *Day of Deceit.* New York: Free Press.

Stolberg, S. 2000. A Genetic Future Both Tantalizing and Disturbing. *New York Times* (1st January), p. C7.

Tagliabue, J. 1996. Pope Bolsters Church's Support for Scientific View of Evolution. *New York Times* (25th October), pp. A1, A4.

Trudeau, G. 2006. Doonesbury. *Duluth News-Tribune* (4 July), p. 6A.

von Eckhardt, B. 1993. *What Is Cognitive Science?* Cambridge, Massachusetts: MIT Press.

Wade, N. 1999. Inside the Cell, Experts See Life's Origin. *New York Times* (6th April), pp. D1, D4.

Webster. 1988. *Webster's New World Dictionary, Third College Edition.* New York: Simon and Schuster.

Weinberg, S. 1977/88. *The First Three Minutes.* New York: Basic Books.

Weinberg. S. 1992. *Dreams of a Final Theory.* New York: Vintage.

Wells, G.A. 1999. *The Jesus Myth.* Chicago: Open Court.

Wheeler, J. 1977. Is Physics Legislated by Cosmology? In R. Duncan and M. Weston-Smith, eds., *The Encyclopedia of Ignorance* (New York: Pocket Books, 1977), pp. 19–35.

White, M. 1999. *Weird Science.* New York: Avon.

Wilford, J.N. 1996a. Found: Most of the Missing Matter Lost Around Edges of Universe. *New York Times* (17th January), pp. A1, A12.

————. 1996b. Life in Space? 2 New Planets Raise Thoughts. *New York Times* (18th January), pp. A1, A12.

————. 1996c. First Branch in Life's Tree was 2 Billion Years Ago. *New York Times* (30th January), pp. B5–B6.

————. 1997. At Other End of 'Big Bang' May Simply Be a Big Whimper. *New York Times* (16th January), pp. A1, A12.

————. 1999a. When No One Read, Who Started to Write? *New York Times* (6th April), pp. D1–D2.

————. 1999b. New Answers to an Old Question: Who Got Here First? *New York Times* (9th November), pp. D1, D4.

Williams, G.C. 1966/96. *Adaptation and Natural Selection*. Princeton: Princeton University Press.

————. 1992. *Natural Selection: Domains, Levels, and Challenges*. New York: Oxford University Press.

Wilson, D.S. 1980. *The Natural Selection of Populations and Communities*. Menlo Park: Benjamin/Cummings.

Wilson, E.O. 1992. *The Diversity of Life*. New York: Norton.

————. 1999. *Consilience: The Unity of Knowledge*. New York: Vintage.

Wolff, E.N. 1996. *Top Heavy*. New York: Free Press.

Wright, R. 1997. *The Moral Animal*. New York: Pantheon.

Yoon, C.K. 1996. Lake Victoria's Lightning-Fast Origin of Species. *New York Times* (27th August), pp. B5–B6.

# Index